Living
Buddhism

Living Buddhism

Andrew Powell

photographs by Graham Harrison

foreword by His Holiness the Dalai Lama

Harmony Books/New York

Half-title page: Butter lamps at a shrine in the precincts of Namgyal monastery, Dharamsala.
Title page: A Tibetan monk with his rosary at the Svayambhūnāth Stupa, Kathmandu, Nepal.
Contents page: The hands of a novice monk during *zazen* at the Japanese Sōtō Zen Monastery of Eiheiji.

Text copyright © 1989 by Andrew Powell
Photographs copyright © 1989 by Graham Harrison

Design by Susan Mann

Published by Harmony Books, a division of Crown Publishers, Inc., 225 Park Avenue South, New York, New York 10003.

Originally published in Great Britain by British Museum Publications Limited.

HARMONY and colophon are trademarks of Crown Publishers, Inc.

Manufactured in Hong Kong

Library of Congress Cataloguing-in-Publication Data

Powell, Andrew.
Living Buddhism.
Bibliography: p.
Includes index.
I. Buddhism. I. Harrison, Graham. II. Title.
BQ4022.P68 1989   294.3   88-32846

ISBN 0-517-57266-4

10 9 8 7 6 5 4 3 2 1

First American Edition

For over two and a half thousand years, different Asian peoples have responded to the teachings of the Buddha in accordance with their various national or cultural dispositions. Now that so many more Westerners are showing an interest in Buddhism, I am delighted to introduce a book which explains the richness and extent of the Buddhist tradition. Buddhism, as this book makes plain, continues to be a powerful spiritual force, uniting people of many nations. Its influence for peace, happiness, and reconciliation is undiminished.

Humanitarian values are the foundations of Buddhism, as I am convinced they are of all great religions. *Living Buddhism* illuminates the human face of the Buddhist tradition, showing the vital role that the Buddha's teaching plays in the lives of his many followers.

Man's inability to control and discipline his mind is responsible for all his problems. Material progress, though often of immense benefit, is no substitute for the age-old spiritual values that have shaped the civilisations of the world. Perhaps today Buddhism may have a part to play in reminding western people of the spiritual dimension of their lives.

I hope this book will stir the imaginations of its readers sufficiently to lead them to discover the full splendour and profundity of the Buddha's teaching.

Tenzin Gyatso, Fourteenth Dalai Lama of Tibet
28 May 1988

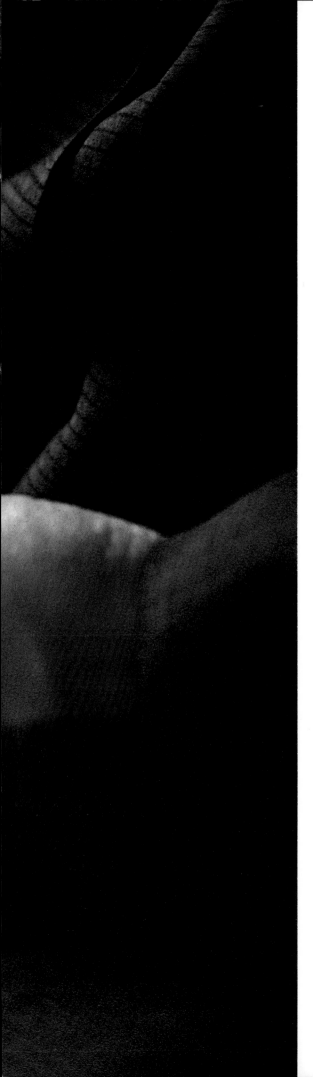

Contents

Author's Preface   9

1 The Noble Path   10

An introduction to the
Buddhist tradition

2 First Principles   42

Theravāda Buddhism in Burma,
Sri Lanka and Thailand

3 The Buddha Mind   78

Japanese paths to Enlightenment

4 An Open Secret   110

Tibetan Buddhism in exile

5 Decline and Destruction   144

The fate of Buddhism
in China and Tibet

6 The Modern Movement   180

Buddhism comes to the West

Map of Buddhist Asia   193

Glossary   195

Bibliography   201

Acknowledgements and Photographic Information   203

Index   205

This is a book intended for the general reader, not for the specialist. It is neither an academic survey nor a manual for the student of oriental philosophy. Its aim is to paint a vivid and memorable portrait of a great and ancient religion, one which today remains of vital importance to hundreds of millions of people. Throughout, the opinions expressed are my own, not those of any other individual or institution.

Living Buddhism came about, somewhat indirectly, as a result of the 1985 British Museum exhibition, *Buddhism – Art and Faith.* In order to provide a setting for the artefacts on display and to supplement the illustration of the catalogue, photographer Graham Harrison was dispatched to the East. Six months later, he returned with over 4,000 transparencies. Clearly, there was no way in which the Museum could do justice to such an abundance of material, so the idea of a book was conceived. Nearly two years later Graham was able to return to Asia, this time accompanied by myself. A further three months' work produced another 6,000 photographs and the substance of the accompanying text. Together we travelled many thousands of miles, researching material in India, Nepal, Sri Lanka, Burma, Thailand, Indonesia, Korea, Japan, China and Tibet.

It has been my ambition to provide a context in which these unique photographs become more than just a succession of strikingly beautiful images. I have therefore endeavoured to combine an explanation of the fundamentals of Buddhist history and philosophy with a report on the present situation, an examination of the developments which affect the religion and its followers in the East today. I have everywhere tried to express myself as simply as possible. Buddhism is a fascinating subject, but it is also a complex one. Certain fundamental ideas – like that of Karma for example – do not readily permit a straightforward explanation. Nonetheless I have sought to hold the attention of the reader who has little previous knowledge of oriental religions, and whose appetite for indigestible chunks of Sanskrit vocabulary is limited.

One of the book's chief merits is, I think, its inclusion of material illustrating all the principal types of Buddhism – notably Theravāda from South-east Asia, Zen from Japan and Tantric Buddhism from Tibet. Because the various Buddhist schools developed so far apart, over such a long period of time, their respective followers tend to have remarkably little knowledge of, and sometimes insufficient respect for, each other's beliefs and practices. As more people in the West are now taking a serious interest in Buddhism, it seems important that we should try not to perpetuate this unfortunate myopia.

No-one who travels in Buddhist lands can remain unaware of the profoundly civilising effect that the religion has had over the centuries. This civilisation is reflected not so much by magnificent architecture and exquisite artistry, but in the attitude of the people; their instinctive gentleness and generosity. I consider myself extremely fortunate to have been able to research and to write *Living Buddhism,* and I very much hope that it is a book which will communicate both my deep respect for Buddhist culture and my great affection for the Buddhist peoples of Asia.

A.P.
London, 1988

*T*he Noble Path

An introduction to the Buddhist tradition

'A heart untouched by worldly things, a heart that is not swayed
By sorrow, a heart passionless, secure – that is the greatest blessing.'   The Buddha, *Sutta Nipāta*

Despite the ravages of the Cultural Revolution, the pitiless wars of South-east Asia and the seemingly irresistible rise of secularism, the observer of Buddhism today is confronted by paradoxical patterns of advance and decline rather than by the widespread diminution of the religion's influence and vitality. True, the Buddhist societies of the East are struggling to negotiate between the conflicting demands of traditional values and those of Western political and social formulas. In consequence Buddhism is often on the defensive, being a religion particularly ill-equipped to contend with the modern imperative of rapid economic growth. Yet in Thailand, for example, while a growing proportion of the population regards Buddhism as irrelevant to its pursuit of higher living standards, some educated city-dwellers are (under the influence of the devout King Bhumibol) once again taking to meditation and devoting time to spiritual practice. Further hope for the future is provided by the Tibetans who, despite all the calamities that the twentieth century has heaped upon them, continue (both in Tibet itself and in exile) to defend their Buddhist culture with heroic tenacity. Though a minor triumph in strictly numerical terms, the return of Buddhism to the heartland of India after an absence of 750 years is also of obvious significance. In the mid 1950s, the lawyer and politician Dr B. R. Ambedkar led groups of 'Untouchables' (the lowest stratum of Indian society, beneath the Hindu caste system) to renounce their former faith and to turn instead to a vision of social justice offered by Buddhism.

Perhaps the most striking evidence that Buddhism continues to be an inexhaustible source of inspiration is the fascination it now holds for the Western world. To many in Europe and America, Buddhism seems to be a religion well suited to mankind's future (as far as we are dimly able to perceive it), being grounded in reason not faith and therefore in harmony with the prevailing spirit of scientific empiricism.

Although offering a path to salvation, Buddhism requires no belief in the suprarational, observing merely that where remarkable men have trodden, it is manifestly reasonable to attempt to follow. Those who encounter its refined morality and profound wisdom can only regard the Buddhist tradition as one of the great achievements of man. It is therefore a reassuring thought that, despite recent reversals of fortune, Buddhism will not merely survive, but may possibly be on the brink of a new age of appreciative revaluation.

The last fifty years have been consistently cruel. In China, Tibet, Mongolia, Vietnam, Laos and Cambodia, regimes inspired by a Western materialist ideology have seen Buddhism as a rival, reactionary force within society, one to be struggled

Buddha image, in the Museum at Sārnāth, north-east India.

Previous page: The Gawdawpalin Temple in Pagan, Burma, built on the banks of the Irrawaddy at the end of twelfth century. Pagan was once one of the great Buddhist cities of Asia and capital of Burma for 250 years.

Dawn at the Buddha's birthplace, Lumbini, Nepal. According to the fifth-century Chinese traveller Fa-hsien, the rectangular pool was where the mother of Buddha bathed before her infant's birth.

against and if possible eradicated. Thousands of monasteries have been closed or demolished and hundreds of thousands of monks imprisoned or murdered. The first great religion to proclaim unequivocally the values of non-violence and unconditional compassion has in the past few decades been afflicted by some of the most brutal persecutions of its long and remarkable history.

Five hundred years older than Christianity, a thousand years older than Islam, Buddhism has of course suffered (and withstood) setbacks before. Most calamitous of these was its disappearance from the land of its origin, India. In 1235, a Tibetan pilgrim visiting the great Buddhist university of Nālandā, found only a single monk and a handful of pupils living a wretched and fearful existence among the ruins of buildings which had once housed ten thousand students from all over Asia. During a long period of decline, Buddhism had increasingly been reassimilated by the Indian tradition from which it had first emerged, a process that came to an abrupt end in the devastation of successive Muslim invasions. Their inhabitants slaughtered, their walls comprehensively shattered, the Buddhist monasteries were never rebuilt. The *Sangha*, the monastic community founded by the Buddha himself, disappeared from India, and his teaching, the *Dharma*, was heard of no more.

By the thirteenth century however, Buddhism had had nearly two millennia in which to become the dominant cultural force of the East. Its path to spiritual fulfilment and its philosophy, morality and aesthetics were regarded with veneration from Sri Lanka to the northern islands of Japan. For a third of the world's people, Buddhism was synonymous with civilisation. And so it remained until the arrival of the Europeans: soldiers, traders, colonial administrators and Christian missionaries.

Fortunately, an early impulse to convert as well as subdue the heathen was not as vigorously pursued as it might have been, and educated Westerners came gradually to acknowledge Buddhism to be not only a religion of great sophistication, but one of

12

exalted ideals, needing no lectures in ethics from heavy-handed evangelists. Radical change had nonetheless become inevitable. Confronted by superior military force, startling technological accomplishment and by energetic conquerors blessed with apparently unshakeable self-confidence, oriental peoples began a period of painful reappraisal during which the very foundations of their respective cultures could not remain exempt from ruthless scrutiny. This revealed that many Eastern societies had become moribund, if not positively corrupt, and that Buddhism – far from being true to its own nature as a religion of individual spiritual effort – had all too often degenerated into institutionalised torpor.

Reactions to these unflattering discoveries varied widely. In Sri Lanka for example, resentment of foreign domination, combined with an awareness of the growing respect of European scholars, led to a vigorous Buddhist revival. Renewed cultural self-esteem quickly became allied to demands for national self-determination, and independence when it came was in no small part due to the vociferous Buddhist clergy. At the same time, Anagārika Dharmapāla, a Sri Lankan of international reputation, campaigned successfully for the restoration of the long-abandoned Buddhist holy places of India. By contrast, attempts to revitalise Buddhism in China gathered little momentum. The humiliation of foreign conquest and the activities of Christian missionaries had prompted a general desire to sweep away the cultural dead wood long before the iconoclasm of Marxist ideologues. The Chinese felt an urgent need to modernise, industrialise and above all to compete on equal terms with the assertive Western powers.

No-one is completely certain when it all began, but it would seem that the man who was to become the Buddha was born in approximately 563 BC at Lumbinī, a village in what is now southern Nepal, close to the Indian border. He lived to the age of eighty and when he died in 483 BC, Pericles was forty-seven years old. Socrates was only six. The future Buddha was given the personal name Siddhārtha in addition to his clan name Gautama. His father was the leader of a people known as the Shākyas and the Buddha is also therefore frequently referred to as Shākyamuni, or 'Sage of the Shākyas'. The title 'Buddha' is itself an honorific meaning 'Awakened One'. This impressive nomenclature not infrequently gives rise to confusion, so it is perhaps worth labouring the point that Prince Siddhārtha, Shākyamuni, the Buddha Gautama and Buddha are all the same person. Siddhārtha was born into the Kshatriya, or warrior caste, and was therefore a distinctly unlikely candidate for sainthood. He was apparently destined to succeed his father as the local chieftain, attended by every luxury readily available in the mid sixth century BC.

Predictably, accounts of the Buddha's life have been richly embellished by legend, but a straightforward biography is to an extent discernible. Although he was an aristocratic young man, affluent, in the best of health and happily married, Siddhārtha became obsessed by an apprehension of life's fundamental inadequacy and an awareness of the ubiquity of human suffering. He therefore determined to abandon home and family, wealth and privilege, in order to seek a solution to these problems. The Ganges plains in north-eastern India were at that time a centre for cultural innovation and dispute, and many teachers and holy men were to be found there, energetically advocating various paths to salvation. They did so in the context of the prevailing Indian orthodoxy, a religious establishment administered and propagated by a priestly caste, the Brahmins. As India is a warm, fertile country, it was quite possible for mendicants and ascetics to survive without permanent shelter or any reliable source of food. Indeed, despite the great changes which have subsequently taken place, many such men still exist in India today. Leaving behind

Left: Surrounded by fields, Bodh Gayā is relatively untroubled by the modern world and its atmosphere still lends itself to calm introspection.

Right: A villager leads his water-buffalo across the river at Bodh Gayā.

comfort and security, Siddhārtha put on the simple yellow robe worn by homeless pilgrims and set off on his spiritual quest. Initially he sought out the most revered religious authorities and, under their guidance, studied philosophy and practised meditation. He was forced to conclude however, that these disciplines could not provide a complete answer to his spiritual dilemma, and he therefore decided to experiment with a life of extreme asceticism. So thorough was his self-denial that, in addition to reducing himself to little more than a breathing skeleton, his hair fell out. Five other ascetics, who had become Siddhārtha's companions, were much impressed by his determination. Understandably, they were somewhat aggrieved to hear him declare that self-mortification had proved to be of little use in his quest for Truth and that he had therefore decided to abandon his austerities.

Having experimented with many forms of spiritual practice and experienced a life of both material gratification and dire poverty, Siddhārtha was obliged to consider what path might now lie open to him. Aware that both indulgence and abstinence were equally futile, he determined to follow a 'middle way' between such extremes and, having washed, rested and eaten, he sat down to meditate beneath a tree at a place now called Bodh Gayā, about fifty miles south of the Ganges in the Indian state of Bihar. Despite being beset initially by doubt and despair, he successfully calmed his mind and eventually, after many hours, came to experience complete illumination: Enlightenment. The emaciated pilgrim had transcended the apparent limitations of human perception and had become the Buddha, the Awakened One.

The Buddha's Enlightenment is the central fact of the Buddhist religion. It is as fundamental as the Crucifixion is to Christianity. The great edifice of Buddhist philosophy and ethics which developed in succeeding centuries could never have been constructed without this one crucial occurrence. So what exactly happened? What is Enlightenment? Unfortunately it is rather difficult to say because it is an experience, one which cannot readily be reduced to the conventional formulas of language. If it could be easily explained, then it would no longer be Enlightenment.

Legend tells us that the Buddha remained in meditation for a period of between a week and two months (accounts differ). Eventually, however, he began to consider whether or not it would be possible to communicate anything of his spiritual insight to others. At first he tended towards the view that his teaching would be impossible to convey, but on further reflection he decided that he should at least make the attempt. Two things seem clear. First, for the remaining forty-five or so years of his life the Buddha never for a moment entertained the slightest doubt about the significance of his experience and secondly, his demeanour and eloquence were sufficiently

Opposite: The twelfth-century Mahabodhi Temple at Bodh Gayā, the site of the Buddha's Enlightenment, and the holiest shrine of the Buddhist world.

Modern Sārnāth. Cyclists commute in the dawn mist. Although one of the four holiest places of Buddhism, Sārnāth, like Bodh Gayā, remains a tranquil backwater.

Previous spread: The Dhamekh stupa in the Deer Park at Sārnāth.

remarkable for him to be able to persuade thousands of people that he had indeed come to understand Reality, despite his inability to explain in so many words exactly what it was. Evidently the Buddha was exceptionally charismatic.

Leaving Bodh Gayā, which is today the chief place of pilgrimage in the Buddhist world, the Buddha made his way to Sārnāth, three or four miles from the great holy city of Varanasi on the banks of the Ganges. There he met the five ascetics whom he had previously so disappointed. Although they did not view his arrival with much enthusiasm, the Buddha was not deterred and proceeded to preach his first, epoch-making sermon on the subject of the 'Four Noble Truths', the analysis of the human condition and the remedy for its ills which lies at the very core of the Buddhist religion. One of the ascetics, Kondañña, quickly realised that although the Buddha had much the same outward appearance as the ragged mendicant Siddhārtha, some kind of complete transformation had clearly taken place. Listening closely to the Buddha's words he began to perceive the truth of his teaching and soon afterwards, acknowledging him as his spiritual preceptor, Kondañña was ordained as the first Buddhist monk, or *bhikkhu*. With little further persuasion, his companions shortly followed his example.

The so-called 'Three Jewels', the three structural pillars of the Buddhist religion, had now all come into being: the 'Buddha', the 'Dharma' (his teaching), and the 'Sangha' (the community of monks who would be its custodians). During the ensuing months, which the Buddha spent at Varanasi, the movement rapidly began to acquire momentum. Later, when he began to travel up and down the Ganges valley, his reputation preceded him: crowds gathered to hear him speak and the wealthy and influential people of the region came to offer material support for the Sangha's activities. Most notable of these benefactors was a banker, Anāthapindika, who donated, at great expense, a pleasure garden known as the Jetāvana Grove in which

the most famous of the early Buddhist monasteries came to be built.

For forty-five years the Buddha preached and argued and exhorted. Eventually, however, he began to weaken and it became necessary to consider exactly how the Sangha would function without his inspiring presence. One of the Buddha's cousins who had joined the Order, an ambitious and unscrupulous man called Devadetta, suggested that a successor should be chosen and that he, Devadetta, was ideally qualified for the position. The Buddha replied that, on the contrary, the Sangha would govern itself; no new leader needed to be selected as, after his death, all decisions were to be taken by a simple majority of the monks present. The Sangha was to be a democratic, not hierarchical institution. In the last months of his life the Buddha emphasised the self-reliance that his monks would require in his absence and, in a famous speech shortly before his death, he gave this instruction its most memorable expression:

'Therefore. . . be islands unto yourselves. Take the Self as your refuge. Take yourself to no external refuge. Hold fast to the Dharma as an island. Hold fast as a refuge to the Truth. . . . And whosoever . . . shall take the Self as an island, taking themselves to no external refuge, but holding fast to the Truth as their refuge, it is they . . . who shall reach the very topmost height. . . .'

Enfeebled by age, the Buddha undertook his final journey accompanied by a group of disciples, including the most solicitous of all his followers, Ānanda, another of his cousins motivated by rather higher principles than Devadetta. Stopping at the town of Pāvā, they went to the house of one of the Buddha's lay followers, who wished to provide them with a meal. Unfortunately, one of the dishes was bad and gave the Buddha food poisoning. His constitution, already debilitated by age and fatigue, was scarcely able to withstand this sudden assault, yet he and Ānanda struggled on to the

19

Left: Kusinārā, northern India. Sri Lankan pilgrims visit the temple built on the site of the Buddha's death.

Right: As with much of the village life of India, little has changed in Kusinārā since the Buddha died.

outskirts of the town of Kusinārā where, between two trees, the Buddha finally lay down on a couch, '. . . on his right side, with one leg resting on the other, mindful and self-possessed'. Ānanda, confronted by the Buddha's impending death, was unable to restrain his grief, but the Buddha, serene despite his physical distress, gently reminded him of the situation's immutable logic:

'Ānanda, do not weep. . . Whatever is born, produced, conditioned, contains within itself the nature of its own dissolution. It cannot be otherwise.'

After having addressed his disciples for the last time and ensured that they had no lingering doubts about the body of teaching that he had left them, the Buddha entered into meditation. The enigma of his death is perhaps most memorably described in the famous scripture, the *Sutta Nipāta:*

> As a flame blown out by the wind
> Goes to rest and cannot be defined
> So the wise man freed from individuality
> Goes to rest and cannot be defined.
> Gone beyond all images –
> Gone beyond the power of words.

The Buddha was dead, but during the four decades of his ministry his Dharma and Sangha had successfully taken root. Gradually, over centuries, Buddhism expanded throughout the Indian sub-continent, coexisting with rather than replacing the ancient Brahminical religion. It spread westwards into areas which are now Pakistan and Afghanistan and on into Iran and Turkestan. During the reign of the great Indian Emperor Aśoka in the third century BC, it moved south, successfully crossing to Sri Lanka where it acquired a permanent sanctuary. Later another Emperor, Kanishka, ruler of the Kushan people in the first century BC, controlled territory stretching from the Indian plains to the Aral Sea in what is now the Soviet Union.

Opposite: Offerings of petals and coins left on a large stone representation of the Buddha's footprints adjacent to the Mahabodhi Temple, Bodh Gayā.

Under his and his successors' patronage, Buddhism enjoyed a golden age, particularly in the Gandhara region to the east of the Khyber Pass in present-day northern Pakistan. It was from the borders of Central Asia that, at the very beginning of the Christian era, Buddhism was carried along the Silk Road into the heartland of China. At approximately the same time it was introduced to the Mon people who then inhabited lands that one day would become Burma and Thailand. In the fourth century it spread to Korea from China and from Korea (in AD 552 we are told) it was taken to Japan where it was halted only by the uncharted expanse of the Pacific. One

hundred years passed before scholars from India, negotiating the Himalayan passes, came at last to the isolated high plateau of Tibet. There, having initially struggled to overcome the indigenous animism, Buddhism was adopted with an exemplary and totally unforeseeable passion. By then however, Muslim armies had already begun to carry the word of the Prophet throughout the lands of the Middle East and Buddhism's western boundaries were becoming increasingly insecure. The eighth century was the first to see Islamic invaders spill down on to the Indian plains. Driven by an alien religious fervour, successive waves of marauders unleashed centuries of intermittent tumult. Buddhism was erased from the land of its origin and a period of expansion which had lasted for 1,500 years finally came to an end.

Despite its independent development in places as far apart as Java and Mongolia, Buddhism is essentially an Indian religion. To the casual observer there may appear to be little similarity between the Buddhism practised in Japan and that in Burma or Thailand, yet beneath the widely differing external forms, there is an irreducible body of doctrine, based on the words of the Buddha himself. More fundamental even than this, however, is the terminology of the religion itself, the framework within which the Buddhist debate takes place. 'Dharma', 'karma', 'nirvāna' are words understood and used by Buddhists everywhere; yet they are not Buddhist in origin, being drawn from the general vocabulary of *Indian* religious experience. The fundamentals of the Buddha's Dharma (as opposed to terms in which they were couched) are nonetheless completely original. The irreducible core of Buddhist teaching is his first sermon, preached to the five ascetics at Sārnāth, and the subject of that sermon, the Four Noble Truths, is nothing less than a distillation of the wisdom which the Buddha had gained through his Enlightenment.

The first Noble Truth is that the basic condition of human existence is *dukkha*, a word usually translated as 'suffering'. Although not denying that life contains the potential for happiness, the Buddha insisted that it was fundamentally unsatisfactory because of its inherent inability to fulfil humanity's spiritual longing. Rather than being a deeply pessimistic analysis leading logically to despair, the Buddha's teaching is that progress and achievement are possible, but only through looking life squarely in the face, and taking the first step on the road to wisdom, which is the recognition of the ubiquity of dukkha. Persisting in delusion will get us absolutely nowhere and, furthermore, make us far more unhappy than if we adopt a more sensible course.

Crucial to the Buddha's understanding of existence was his acceptance of the prevalent ideas of *karma* and rebirth. The traditional Indian view, which the Buddha endorsed, was that human beings are trapped in an endless cycle of lives known as *samsāra*. There is no easy escape from dukkha because the consequences of all one's previous actions, a residuum known as karma, survive the death of the body to condition a new physical existence. The Buddha did *not* maintain that a particular individual is reborn, indeed he insisted both that all things are subject to the law of mutability (known in Buddhism as *anicca*), and that there is no such thing as a personal entity or soul, a doctrine known as *anattā*, or 'no-self'. However karma, which may perhaps best be understood as a package of energy composed of both morally positive and negative charges, is transferable from one life to the next.

The second Noble Truth is that dukkha has an identifiable cause. This cause is *tanhā*, which is generally translated as 'desire', but which has, in common with dukkha, a whole gamut of meanings including an incorrigible tendency to seek satisfaction in the objects of the senses and a desperate will to live unrelated to any serious or systematic attempt to understand what life actually involves. Fortunately, the third Noble Truth is that tanhā, the cause of suffering, can be eliminated and therefore that escape from the cycle of rebirth is possible after all. The fourth Noble

23

A 2000-year-old stupa at Sāñcī, central India. The stupa is the most distinctive form of Buddhist architecture.

Truth is that the way to salvation, to Nirvāna, has been identified by the Buddha and set out as the Noble Eightfold Path.

The subject matter of the Eightfold Path falls into three sections dealing in turn with Wisdom, Morality and Meditation. The first step on the Path is 'Right Understanding', making it plain at the outset that in Buddhism faith alone is insufficient and that spiritual progress should be based primarily on a determined effort to understand the Dharma. The second of the eight steps is 'Right Thought', which means 'correct motivation', the Buddha clearly wishing to stress that his programme for spiritual progress should not be followed out of a desire for self-aggrandisement.

Having outlined the essential components of wisdom, the Eightfold Path now turns its attention to morality. The Third Step, 'Right Speech', requires not merely a scrupulous attention to the truth but also a controlled attitude to the world. A careful choice of words reflects mental refinement and also involves a recognition that words are in effect deeds. The Fourth Step, 'Right Action', indicates what, for a Buddhist, constitutes moral behaviour. At the most elementary level, Buddhism has five precepts known as the *Pancha Sila* and these everyone, whether monk or layman, must undertake to observe. They are 1) Do not kill (an injunction which applies to *all* forms of life, not merely human beings); 2) Do not steal; 3) Do not give way to sexual incontinence (for the layman, adultery and promiscuity; monks are generally expected to be celibate and chaste); 4) Do not tell lies; 5) Do not take any form of intoxicant (as this destroys mental control and equilibrium). The importance for a Buddhist of earning a living in a manner which is generous in spirit, non-exploitative, and which does not involve compromise with the Pancha Sila (for example, by taking animal life), is stressed in the Fifth Step, 'Right Livelihood'. The last step on the Path which falls under the heading of 'Morality' is 'Right Effort'. The Buddha intended his

path to be one of strenuous and unremitting commitment. It demands sustained exertion to subdue the passions and control the mind, an exacting determination to come to terms with the limitations of our humanity in the unwavering pursuit of spiritual liberation.

The final two steps on the Noble Eightfold Path – 'Right Mindfulness' and 'Right Concentration' – refer specifically to the techniques of mental control, or meditation, which enable the Buddhist not merely to understand the Buddha's teaching but to perceive its truth directly. Buddhist meditation may be divided into two distinct categories: *samatha* and *vipassanā*. Samatha, which means 'tranquillity', involves directing attention to a single object of contemplation. Normally the mind flits randomly from object to object. It is undisciplined and, as a tool for the perception of spiritual truth, quite useless. Samatha teaches us therefore how to focus our minds precisely. When skill in the development of concentration has been achieved, mental tranquillity is the result, and increasingly refined states of consciousness may be attained.

Vipassanā, or 'Insight' meditation, is rather different. Although the practitioner may begin by generating concentration through samatha, he then permits the mind free rein and allows it to focus on whatever it chooses. The subconscious (to employ modern terminology) is thereby brought within the scope of conscious awareness. Later the mind may be given a specific subject to dwell upon, such as an aspect of the Buddha's teaching, the object being to bring about a direct realisation of its truth, as opposed to a simple understanding of its assertions. Techniques of meditation have reached their greatest complexity in the Tibetan Tantric tradition: mandalas (sacred diagrams) are employed to guide the meditator and a highly elaborate method known as 'Deity Yoga' has been developed to control and harness the human passions.

Security guard at the greatest of all Buddhist monuments: the ninth-century stupa of Borobudur, Java. The Borobudur complex forms a vast three-dimensional mandala.

Following spread: Relief at Borobudur of the Buddha preaching his first sermon at Sārnāth.

25

Whatever the precise nature of the meditation practice, however, the ultimate aim is the same: serene realisation of that which lies beyond concepts and beyond words. The eighth and final step of the Path, *Sammā Samādhi*, or 'Right Concentration', directs us to this end, pointing to a destination where rules and formulas have long been transcended and where the Buddha's teaching is reintegrated in the mind of Enlightenment. Through meditation the Buddhist hopes to gain more and more frequent glimpses of the Truth, until one day he is able to sustain the vision, to live within this Higher Reality. Such is the achievement of the *arhat*, one who has travelled the Path, reached the goal and attained Nirvāna. Of Nirvāna the Buddha is recorded as saying:

'There is a sphere which is neither earth, nor water, nor fire, nor air, which is not the sphere of the infinity of space, nor the sphere of the infinity of consciousness, the sphere of nothingness, the sphere of perception, or non-perception, which is neither this world nor the other world, neither sun nor moon. I deny that it is coming or going, enduring, death, or birth. It is only the end of suffering.'

This then is the Noble Eightfold Path, the last of the Four Noble Truths, which together form the substance of the Buddha's first sermon and the vital core of Buddhist belief. These fundamentals of the Dharma are today accorded the same veneration in Bangkok and Colombo as they are in Lhasa and Kyoto. Centuries of independent development in regions separated by thousands of miles has led to great diversity within the Buddhist tradition and at first sight this can seem bewildering to Westerners accustomed to religion administered by a strong, centralised authority. Nonetheless, despite their lack of uniformity, all Buddhist schools share the same foundations, being immovably grounded in the first principles of the Indian religion.

Immediately following the Buddha's death, an understandable degree of unanimity prevailed among his disciples and their descendants, but after a century or so the first differences of interpretation and emphasis started to appear. The Buddha himself had not proposed any consistent system of philosophy or metaphysics, being concerned only with the practical business of spiritual liberation, but before long members of the Sangha busied themselves making good his omission. The body of theory and commentary which evolved came to be known as *Abhidhamma*, or 'Higher Dharma'. Rapidly, Buddhism began to acquire schools centred around points of contention. Eighteen of these are said to have arisen in India before the momentous development which began to transform Buddhism around the beginning of the Christian era: the rise of the *Mahāyāna*.

The eighteen early Indian Buddhist schools are known collectively as the *Hīnayāna*, a pejorative term meaning 'Lesser Vehicle' (of salvation), which was bestowed on them by the schools of the Mahāyāna, or self-proclaimed 'Greater Vehicle'. The only one of these which now survives is the *Theravāda*, and it is Buddhism of this type which is found today in Sri Lanka, Burma and Thailand. All other Buddhist schools – those found for example in Tibet, China, and Japan – belong to the *Mahāyāna*.

Theravāda means 'Doctrine of the Elders', the 'Elders' being the group of the Buddha's disciples who, immediately following his death, convened the First Great Council. The purpose of this was to recite the Buddha's teachings, in order to agree upon a definitive version. The time for argument and debate was over. The forty years of his ministry had been sufficient to convince them of the completeness and perfection of his doctrine. Now their task was the protection and dissemination of that uniquely precious legacy. For the next twenty-five centuries the emphasis in Theravāda Buddhism would be not on philosophical interpretation, but on discipline. Of course Theravāda did not literally come into existence at the First Council. Not until disagreements arose would anyone think in terms of different schools, or of an orthodoxy which required to be kept pure, free from harmful innovation.

So what precisely did the Elders agree to be the foundation of their religion? The answer is that no-one can be absolutely sure. This is simply because the Buddha himself wrote nothing and his teaching was not written down in its entirety until four hundred years after his death. Tradition would have us believe that three of the Buddha's chief disciples had memorised the three sections into which Theravāda canonical literature is now divided. According to some accounts, Ānanda is said to have recited the *Sutta-pitaka* (sermons), Upali the *Vinaya-pitaka* (discipline), and Kassapa the *Abhidhamma-pitaka* (metaphysics, philosophy and psychology). Unfortunately these neat classifications are undoubtedly a later, literary invention. On the other hand, the fact that the Buddha's words were not recorded does not mean that they were forgotten. Today in the Far East there are still monks who can recite a substantial proportion of the Theravāda scriptures (the complete Thai edition fills forty-five volumes), and the oral tradition in India was undoubtedly carried on by men of similar ability. This huge body of knowledge was probably transmitted from generation to generation with a remarkable degree of accuracy. Though much of the Abhidhamma was certainly composed at a much later date, both the Suttas and Vinaya lead directly back to the First Council and may indeed contain the actual words of the Buddha himself.

It was the Vinaya, or Discipline, which established the parameters of early Buddhism, and which, in theory at least, has governed the Theravāda school ever since. Theravāda monks submit to 227 rules of conduct which contain precise instructions about all aspects of the religious life. They are, for example, required to beg for their food, to abstain from eating after midday and to own no more than eight specified possessions: namely a three-part robe, a loin cloth, a begging bowl, a water strainer, a razor and a needle. From an acquaintance with these rules it is not difficult to understand the nature of the original Buddhist Sangha.

The code of morality and conduct which lies at the very heart of Theravāda Buddhism is one for *monastic* life. It contains little which is addressed to the layman. Both in early Buddhism and in Theravāda today, the religious life is quite clearly regarded as in every way superior to that of the ordinary citizen. Indeed to have any hope of making any real progress, let alone of achieving Nirvāna, one must become a monk. In essence, Theravāda Buddhism is a religion for those who have renounced the world, and the Vinaya (Discipline) explicitly sets out to prevent monks from becoming entangled in worldly affairs: they are not allowed to work, to have money, to cook their own food, or to live under the same roof as a woman.

The Theravāda Sangha is intended to be a spiritual brotherhood, collective strength enabling the individual to pursue a severe and narrow path to his own salvation. The spiritual quest is therefore essentially self-centred. One becomes a monk for one's own benefit, not in order to be useful in society. Of course there is a relationship between the Sangha and society, but it is a subtle one. As long as a monk has to beg for his food, he can never be completely independent and his daily appearance on his alms round serves as a spiritual and moral example to all who see him pass. Giving alms is an obviously generous thing to do and in this way the monk also provides the occasion for virtue.

Just as they had before the death of the Buddha, the original Sangha continued to wander the plains of northern India, seeking whatever refuge they could, taking whatever food they were given and, although not actively seeking physical austerity, nonetheless living a life of great simplicity and self-denial. Only in the monsoon season when the Ganges flooded and the ground was swamped were they directed by the

Edict from the great Buddhist Emperor Aśoka of India. Carved onto a pillar at Sārnāth in the third century BC it instructs monks and laymen not to create schisms within the Buddhist faith.

Opposite:
Buddhas in the inner shrine of one of the caves at Ajaṇṭā. Intended to reinforce the worshipper's faith the multiplied Buddha image is a characteristic of early Buddhist art.

Left: Buddha in one of the seventh-century rock temples at Ellora, near Ajaṇṭā, in western India. Ellora was completed at the end of the great age of Buddhist cave temple architecture in India.

Right: Ruins of the monks' cells at the great monastic university of Nālanda, north-east India. In its heyday in the seventh century, Nālanda housed 10,000 students from all over Asia.

Vinaya to find a retreat and temporarily to abandon their peripatetic ways. This then is the ideal, that of the religious mendicant, which exists beneath the massive superstructure of all later Buddhist thought and practice.

Far from being the result of schism, or any form of dramatic upheaval, Mahāyāna Buddhism evolved gradually, over a period of hundreds of years. When the famous Chinese pilgrim and traveller Hsüan-tsang visited India in the seventh century, he estimated that there were approximately 115,000 Hīnayāna and 120,000 Mahāyāna monks, though half of the latter also studied Hīnayāna scriptures. Both Hīnayāna and Mahāyāna monks observed the same code of discipline and considered themselves to be members of an undivided Sangha.

Due to the course accidentally taken by colonial history, it was Hīnayāna (Theravāda) Buddhism in South-east Asia which was first encountered and extensively studied by Europeans. In consequence, there is a lingering tendency in the West to regard this form of the religion as 'the real thing' and Mahāyāna as a later aberration, a corruption of the Buddha's Dharma which took place chiefly in China

and Japan. Such invidious comparisons are unfortunate. As Hsüan-tsang's statistics clearly show, Mahāyāna Buddhism flourished on Indian soil side by side with the schools of the Hīnayāna, the two movements being compatible from the beginning.

Of the fundamental differences in outlook which distinguish the Hīnayāna from the Mahāyāna, perhaps the single most important concerns their respective attitudes towards the Buddha himself. Hīnayāna schools placed great emphasis on the events of the Buddha's life and their scriptures claimed to record his actual words. Although Mahāyāna Buddhism has equal veneration for the Buddha and his Dharma, the movement has devoted much of its energy to considering the Buddha's role as the representative of a transcendent principle, rather than concentrating on his life as an exemplary human being. When the Buddha achieved Enlightenment, he is said to have understood the nature of the Ultimate Reality, and in that realisation to have become, in some ineffable sense, co-extensive with it. But what is the nature of this Reality? What is the goal of the Buddhist spiritual quest? Such questions, held to be unprofitable, if not futile, in early Buddhism, are the life-blood of the Mahāyāna tradition. In pursuit of satisfactory answers, it steadily constructed a vast edifice of literature and philosophy – in Sanskrit, Chinese, Japanese and Tibetan. Both Hīnayāna and Mahāyāna Buddhism seek to recommend a path to salvation, but whereas the former may be characterised as being practical and straightforward, the Mahāyāna is elaborate, speculative, poetic and mystical.

A logical consequence of regarding the Buddha primarily as the representative of

Opposite: Fresco of the Bodhisattva Padmapani, the 'Lotus Born', in one of the cave temples of Ajaṇṭā.

cosmic Truth is the denial of his uniqueness. Mahāyāna views the Buddha as merely one of innumerable manifestations of the Universal Absolute which have occurred over an incomprehensible period of time. As a result of this point of view, it has conceived of other imaginary Buddhas, the most frequently encountered being *Amitābha* (Amida in Japanese), the 'Buddha of Boundless Light' who is said to live in the paradise of *Sukhāvatī*. Confronted by an alarming proliferation of religious *dramatis personae*, it is only too easy to assume that Mahāyāna Buddhism has replaced an austere and rational creed with a hotch-potch of improbable deities. In fact this 'mythology' is, at its most exalted, simply an attempt to engineer an approach to the ineffable Absolute. The Buddha Amitābha, for example, may be regarded as the Higher Self and his paradise as *Bodhi-citta*, the 'Wisdom-heart', which may be awakened in the mind of man.

On the other hand, there is no doubt that the creation of a colourful pantheon has had, over the centuries, the effect of recommending Mahāyāna Buddhism to a large, insufficiently educated lay congregation. Buddhism had long stressed the superiority of monastic life and, while encouraging religious effort by the laity, it generally made little secret of its opinion that significant spiritual progress could be achieved only with a level of dedication impossible outside the walls of a monastery. It was an arduous, intellectually demanding religion, in many ways unlikely to prove attractive to a mass following. However, having acquired a celestial hierarchy, Mahāyāna Buddhism found itself rather better equipped to rival the devotional cults of Hinduism, not to mention the battalions of spirits and demons in animist folk religions. One of the most extreme examples of Mahāyāna popularisation was the eventual elevation of the Buddha Amitābha by the Chinese (and subsequently Japanese) Pure Land School to the rank of saviour. To ensure rebirth in his paradise, Sukhāvatī, all that was required it was claimed, was sufficient faith in Amitābha's compassion and his talents as a redeemer. Despite frequent assertions to the contrary, the enduring enthusiasm for Pure Land Buddhism suggests that the majority of its followers choose to interpret this doctrine quite literally, rather than in an esoteric sense, symbolically.

Such radical departures from the stern first principles of Buddhism should doubtless be understood as consequences merely of the Mahāyāna's uncontrolled fecundity. Far more important overall is the radically different attitude of Mahāyāna Buddhism to worldly life exemplified by its 'bodhisattva ideal', another crucial difference in emphasis distinguishing it from the Hīnayāna schools. The exemplary figure of early Buddhism is the *arhat*, the individual who, rejecting the world, achieves individual salvation by his own efforts. That of the Mahāyāna, on the other hand, is the *bodhisattva*, the man who having reached the supreme spiritual pinnacle opts, of his own free will, to remain within the cycle of rebirth in order to promote the Buddha's Dharma and to help others along the path to Enlightenment. Characteristic of the Mahāyāna then is the promotion of the virtue of compassion, *karunā*. Whereas the Hīnayāna schools had stressed wisdom, *prajñā*, the Mahāyāna saw the combination of wisdom and compassion as the supreme ideal. Thus the world, as the theatre of religious action, was subtly revalued.

Although Mahāyāna developed slowly and organically out of early Buddhism, expanding and refining its doctrines over centuries, it would be wrong to infer that the movement was without prominent innovators or critical turning-points in its long and complex history. Indeed the whole edifice may be seen as one resting on two gigantic pillars, two seminal philosophies. The first of these, known as *Mādhyamika*, arose in the second century AD and was the creation of one of the most influential of all Indian thinkers, Nāgārjuna. Mādhyamika means 'Middle Doctrine', and its name must not be confused with the 'middle way' between indulgence and asceticism which the Buddha identified before his Enlightenment. Nāgārjuna's philosophy rested on a ruthless system of analysis by which he sought to discredit all intellectual concepts which had previously been held to be descriptive of spiritual truth. Taking pairs of opposites such as 'unity and diversity', 'annihilation and permanence', he set out to show that nothing ultimately meaningful could be expressed by such terms and that therefore Reality must reside somewhere in the middle, between extremes. This mystical, inexpressible middle ground he described as 'Emptiness' or *Shūnyatā*.

Two centuries after Nāgārjuna, two brothers, Asanga and Vasubandhu, began the second great philosophical tradition of the Mahāyāna: the *Yogācāra*. Whereas Mādhyamika had concentrated on an intellectual investigation into the nature of reality, Yogācāra was far more directly concerned with psychology and with the insights that might be gained through meditation. The fundamental assertion of the Yogācāra School was that everything is merely the manifestation of universal Mind and that therefore the subject-object duality which mankind presumes to exist between his consciousness and the world is an illusion. All things that are ultimately real are in fact undifferentiated, and through meditation this unity may be directly experienced.

Clearly, the speculations of Mādhyamika and Yogācāra philosophy are not susceptible to concise and accurate summary. In a brief survey of the evolution of Buddhism, it is perhaps sufficient to state baldly that the ideas developed by the two schools were integral to the entire subsequent history of the Mahāyāna. They provided the intellectual and spiritual foundations on which its golden ages in seventh-century China, twelfth-century Japan and fourteenth-century Tibet came in turn to be built. The Tantric Buddhism of the Tibetan Himalaya and the Zen Buddhism of the Kyoto sand garden, utterly dissimilar though they superficially appear to be, are in fact indissolubly linked by a shared lineage which began in the great monastic universities of northern India.

The creative ferment which Mahāyāna ideas brought about in India found its chief expression in the composition of long, ornate sūtras, the vast majority of which were, mostly for form's sake, put into the mouth of the Buddha himself. In contrast to the suttas of the Hīnayāna schools, which were based on an oral tradition allegedly relaying what the Buddha actually said, those of the Mahāyāna were a combination of philosophy, religious theory and imaginative literature. Unsurprisingly, the lack of mystery surrounding the circumstances under which they were written has not prevented people from insisting that they have a genuine historical provenance. It has often been maintained that the Buddha instructed his disciples to hide copies of his most complex teachings, which then came to light centuries later when mankind had developed sufficiently to be able to understand the profundities they contained.

Two of the greatest Mahāyāna sūtras, the *Lankāvatāra Sūtra* and the *Avatamsaka Sūtra*, were in fact directly related to the Yogācāra School. These, and other works like them, were later carried haphazardly along the trade routes, or deliberately transported in the saddle baggage of scholars and pilgrims, until eventually the ideas of Indian Mahāyāna Buddhism had been disseminated throughout the whole of northern Asia. The Avatamsaka Sūtra for example, was first taken to China where it became the chief text of the Hua-yen school. This in turn was shipped to Japan where it was known as the Kegon school. Although the extent of the Mahāyāna scriptures is vast, certain other sūtras stand out as being of pre-eminent importance. Of these, the *Saddharma-pundarika*, or 'Lotus Sūtra' and the *Prajñā-pāramitā*, or 'Perfection of Wisdom', literature take pride of place. The latter is especially significant as among its 125,000 verses are two famous epitomes of its teachings, the *Heart Sūtra* and the *Diamond Sūtra*, which for the past 1,600 years have remained among the most popular

and widely read of all Mahāyāna Buddhist texts.

The great, continuing mystery of Buddhism is why the unprecedented creative impetus of the Indian Mahāyāna schools apparently contained within itself the seeds of its own destruction. Buddhism in India was finally obliterated by Moslim armies, but there is little doubt that the religion was already well advanced in decline. The slaughter and destruction of conquest abruptly halted its accelerating slide to the margins of Indian cultural life. Buddhism was certainly not singled out by the Islamic invaders for particularly savage repression. Hinduism received exactly the same treatment, yet the Hindu temples were rebuilt and the religion survived with both its philosophical tradition and the vigour of its popular support intact. Various attempts have been made to account for the process of degeneration which seems to have affected Indian Buddhism from about the sixth century onwards, but a straight-forward, uncontroversial explanation has yet to be agreed upon.

Certainly, as time went by, the Mahāyāna increasingly replaced Hīnayāna Buddhism on the Indian mainland, leaving Sri Lanka as the stronghold of the older, more austere Theravāda tradition. This was in itself no reason for the onset of decline. However, allied to this gradual transformation seems to have been an increasing readiness to accede to lay demands that Buddhism should become a popular religion with the associated paraphernalia of devotional cults and shoals of subsidiary godlings. Later Mahāyāna began to absorb and adapt many Hindu elements and at the same time the frontiers of Mahāyāna speculative thought increasingly coincided with those of Hindu metaphysics and mysticism. The results of this process may today be clearly seen among the Newar people of Nepal's Kathmandu Valley, whose religion is a peculiar combination of Hinduism and Buddhism, probably quite similar to late Indian Mahāyāna.

The most disputed aspect of this reassimilation is the role played in it by a group of scriptures known as the *Tantras*, which were written in India and widely distributed from the seventh century AD onwards. Certain scholars have declared that the demise of Indian Buddhism became inevitable as soon as its essentially rational tradition allowed itself to be compromised by esoteric tantric practices which were entangled with the occult and anyway entirely of Hindu origin. This point of view is vehemently denied by Tibetan Buddhism which insists not only that there are strictly Buddhist Tantras untainted by Hinduism, but also that they describe (albeit cryptically) the most powerful and effective forms of spiritual practice available to the seeker after Truth. Tibetans refer to the adoption and refinement of Tantric practices as the 'Third turning of the Wheel of the Dharma'. Just as the Hīnayāna was immeasurably extended by the Mahāyāna, so they claim Tantrayāna transformed the Mahāyāna by providing techniques of previously undreamed-of efficacy for the attainment of Enlightenment. Tibetan Buddhists consider that they inherited the culmination of the Indian tradition and that it was their libraries which preserved the final and most remarkable flowering of Buddhism from the depredations of the Islamic invaders.

Precisely where the truth resides between these clearly incompatible points of view it is extremely difficult to discover. It may be said with confidence however, that although Buddhism seems to have degenerated in India prior to its extinction, Tibetan Buddhism as it is presently practised is certainly not a degenerate religion. Indeed the great lamas who today surround the Dalai Lama are undeniably some of the most impressive figures in the Buddhist world, being distinguished by their conspicuous erudition and great religious conviction.

Speculation about the decline of Indian Buddhism, though not leading to a great many incontestable conclusions, does nonetheless serve to focus attention once again on the precarious relationship between monastic Buddhism and that of the laity.

Previous spread: Preaching Buddha guarded by a bodhisattva. Chiselled from solid rock as an act of faith, the cave temples of Ellora stand testimony to the power Buddhism once had in India.

Buddhism is a particularly difficult religion to promote among the population as a whole, without betraying its rigorous and refined ideals. Ultimately it is the Sangha which maintains the religion's integrity. Yet the Sangha cannot exist forever in isolation; it grows out of, and is supported by, lay society. The detached observer of Buddhism in the East today cannot fail to notice the increasing gulf between an often vigorous monastic tradition and the bulk of the lay congregation, dissatisfied with traditional cultural forms and lured into secularism by improvements in the material standard of living.

Much of the problem nowadays stems from the fact that Buddhism as it has been popularly practised has often been a fairly unremarkable mixture of raw superstition and immemorial animism. Images and relics of the Buddha Shākyamuni have been worshipped just as unthinkingly in the Theravāda countries of South-east Asia, as have the ranks of Buddhas and bodhisattvas in the Mahāyāna lands north of the Himalayas. The challenge presently confronting Buddhism is to introduce an increasingly educated and affluent lay population to the fundamental nobility of their religion and to make plain its compatibility with the prevailing spirit of the age. Without a sustained attempt to win back allegiance, the Sangha is in danger of becoming ever more peripheral to the developing societies of the East. In the past fifty years the forces of ideological materialism have brought mayhem to many of the Buddhist lands of Asia, yet ultimately it may be the technological materialism of the West, rather than the tyranny of the Red Guards or the Khmer Rouge, which proves more inimical to Buddhism's ancient hegemony.

In a narrative relief from Borobudur the Buddha's teaching, the Dharma, is carried by sea to other lands.

Following spread: A line of meditating Buddhas at Ellora.

*F*irst Principles

Theravāda Buddhism in Burma, Sri Lanka and Thailand

'Men who have not observed proper discipline, and have not gained wealth in their youth, perish like old herons in a lake without fish.'
The Dhammapada

Glowing in the sunshine, the great golden stupa of the Shwedagon still commands the skyline of Rangoon – no vainglorious architect has yet usurped the pre-eminence of the city's temples. It is difficult to say precisely how old the Shwedagon is, as it has been rebuilt several times. Allegedly, like many ancient structures elsewhere in India, Nepal and Sri Lanka, it was erected over relics of the Buddha; in this case eight of his hairs. What is scarcely in doubt, however, is its eloquence as a symbol. The gleaming tower speaks unmistakably of the transformation that, throughout the centuries, has overtaken Theravāda Buddhism. Covered with gold (the top of the tower is also encrusted with diamonds and rubies and capped with one gigantic emerald), the Schwedagon tells of a religion that is now grand, influential and established; not so much the faith of humble mendicants as a power in the land. It might be held that the Shwedagon's magnificence is symbolic only of the glory of the Buddha's Dhamma and that the gifts of gold and jewels, donated by pious Burmese, are simply extensions of the humble offerings of rice and vegetables given daily to the monks on their alms round. There may even be some justice in this point of view, but the history of Theravāda Buddhism also permits another interpretation.

Many of the very first Buddhist buildings were probably erected at, or near, sites associated with the monsoon retreat. The Indian rainy season annually made travel impossible, so the Buddha's followers were obliged to shelter near villages until the weather improved and they could resume their wandering. The sense of community, of shared ideals, which these enforced periods of sedentary life encouraged was soon augmented with practical support, thanks to fields and buildings donated by the villagers. Rapidly Buddhism developed into a monastic religion based on permanent institutions and although the strict rules governing a monk's possessions remained in force, the Sangha collectively became a landowner. For about two hundred years this parochial arrangement of monks and laymen flourished, modestly, in northern India. Buddhism was however just one religious group among many and by no means the largest; it was the influence of a single man which utterly transformed Buddhism's destiny.

In the third century BC one of the greatest and most powerful of all Indian empires arose on the Ganges plains. Its ruler, Aśoka, controlled the greater part of the Indian sub-continent. However, after a period of ruthless conquest, Aśoka chose, with remarkable abruptness, to renounce warfare and to become Buddhist. Far from being merely a matter of political expedience, his conversion to Buddhism seems to have been motivated by spiritual conviction. He humbly referred to himself as an *upāsaka*,

Opposite: Burma's most venerated shrine, the golden stupa of the Shwedagon in Rangoon. Rising to over 320ft, the Shwedagon is said to house eight of the Buddha's hairs.

2

or lay follower of the Dhamma. Throughout his vast possessions, he ordered columns to be erected, engraved on which were the moral precepts of the religion, and he began to formulate imperial policies in accordance with strict Buddhist ideals. He built hospitals, dug wells and restricted the killing of animals for food. He is also said to have insisted on the purification of the Sangha, expelling those monks whose adherence to the rules of the Vinaya had become less than entirely scrupulous. During the long period of Aśoka's benevolent rule, the foundations were laid for Buddhism to become a world religion.

Though the immediate effects of his actions were almost wholly positive, Aśoka's remarkable achievements were to have side effects which could scarcely have been foreseen. Most importantly he had demonstrated that, however unworldly a religion Buddhism might be, the spread of its doctrine was inevitably bound up with prevailing political circumstances. In addition he had created the archetype of the virtuous Buddhist ruler: an ideal combination of secular and spiritual authority. From now on, in the name of the Dhamma, kings would concern themselves with the Sangha and the Sangha would hanker after political power.

Despite being Buddhism's greatest evangelist, Aśoka was tolerant of other religions. Although he dispatched missionaries to neighbouring countries, he never tried to compel his own subjects to abandon other beliefs. With hindsight we can now see that his greatest triumph was sending his son, Mahinda, on a mission to Sri Lanka where he successfully converted the king, the nobility and, indirectly, the people. As a result Sri Lanka became the first Buddhist state, preserving and disseminating the Theravāda tradition after its disappearance from the mainland of India.

Left: The shrine of the Bo-tree, Anurādhapura, Sri Lanka. The holy tree was grown from a cutting taken in BC 236 from the Bo-tree at Bodh Gayā. Although only a fragment of the original tree survives, it is now surrounded by its flourishing descendants.

Right: A pilgrim prays before the Bo-tree at Anurādhapura.

Much of the prestige which has historically been accorded to the Sinhalese Sangha is due to the Theravāda Canon, the *Tipitaka*, having first been written down under its supervision. This milestone in Buddhist history was, however, reached in rather an unlikely manner. King Tissa, converted by Aśoka's son Mahinda, was kind to his adopted religion and during his reign the Mahāvihāra monastery, for centuries the centre of Theravāda orthodoxy, was built in his capital. The future of Buddhism in Sri Lanka now looked relatively secure, but immediately following Tissa's death in 207 BC, the island was invaded by Tamils from southern India. Their occupation lasted for over a century. During this time Buddhism became explicitly associated with Sinhalese nationalism; one king even went so far as to carry a relic of the Buddha into battle on his spear, an identification of the Sangha with the state which has persisted until the present day. It was in response to this turbulent era, and a general sense of impending calamity, that the Tipitaka was set down, sometime in the first century BC.

Opposite: An offering of a flower in the hand of one of the 'Sigirya Damsels', a detail from the brilliantly painted frescoes in the citadel palace of the fifth-century Sinhalese King, Kasyapa.

Local villagers come to listen to a forest monk's advice after the death of one of their relatives. Island Hermitage, Dondanduwa, Sri Lanka.

Theravāda canonical literature is written in Pāli, the Indian language considered by Theravādins to have been spoken by the Buddha. (In fact he probably spoke a dialect.) As a literary language, Pāli has played in the cultures of South-east Asia a role similar to that of Latin in those of western Europe. Tipitaka means 'three baskets', this expression referring to the grouping of the canonical texts into three collections: Vinaya, Sutta and Abhidhamma. By far the largest of these is the Sutta-pitaka which is further subdivided into five *nikāyas*. The suttas, although very repetitive, a legacy of the oral tradition, contain memorable poetry as well as moral instruction. They take the form of discourses, reported by the Buddha's disciples, at the end of which the listener acknowledges the truth of the Buddha's exposition and asks to be admitted to the ranks of his followers. It is here that exact phrases used by the Buddha himself are very probably preserved. One hundred and twelve short pieces in a section of one of the Nikāyas known as the *Itivuttaka* are considered to be entirely the Buddha's own words. The most famous and widely read section of the Sutta-pitaka, is the *Dhammapada*, 426 verses presenting Buddhist ethics in a poetic and accessible style. Although there are no grounds for direct comparison, the Dhamma-pada is as central to the life of a devout Theravāda Buddhist as the Gospels to a Christian, or the Bhagavad ḡitā to a Hindu.

Despite the incalculable contribution of the Tipitaka to the development of the Theravāda tradition, the two thousand years of the Sinhalese Sangha's subsequent history were not greatly distinguished by their serenity, or even, for extended periods, by their piety. On three occasions – in the eleventh, fifteenth and eighteenth centuries

– the ordination lineage has lapsed and monks have been summoned from Burma (twice) and Thailand to restore the succession. One of the reasons for this surprising frailty has been a consistent inability to separate religion from worldly affairs. This failing was demonstrated as recently as 1959, when the Sinhalese Prime Minister, Mr S.W.R.D. Bandaranaike, was assassinated by a Buddhist monk, having three years earlier been elected with the enthusiastic support of the clergy. From the very beginning, the Sangha received generous gifts of property and, by about the tenth century, it had become the largest landowner in the whole country. Buddhism had been introduced to Sri Lanka through its nobility; it continued to be patronised by the nobility and indeed many noblemen became monks. Prominent members of the Sangha were therefore related to prominent members of the government and, far from engendering an ideal Buddhist society on an Aśokan pattern, it led to an unholy alliance dedicated to the maintenance of prestige and power. The growing wealth of the Sangha also led to the construction of ever more grandiose religious buildings in the cities of Anurādhapura, Polonnaruwa and Kandy. Ironically the hall of residence in a Sinhalese monastery is known as the *pansala*, which originally meant 'house of leaves'. This term, as well as the Pāli word for a monk – *bhikkhu*, a mendicant – is a reminder of an earlier and altogether different tradition.

It would of course be completely wrong to infer from this erosion of ideals that the Sinhalese Sangha produced no remarkable or holy men in a little over two thousand years. For much of the time there were numbers of forest bhikkhus who lived in conditions of great simplicity and who in consequence were much venerated by the

Meditation at Dondanduwa on the transience of human life.

The Gal Vihera,
Polonnaruwa, Sri Lanka,
depicting Ānanda, the
Buddha's faithful
disciple, and the Buddha
himself reclining on his
death-bed.

Opposite: A young
Sinhalese monk absorbed
in his studies in the city
of Kandy. A long
established centre of
learning, Kandy now
maintains the traditions
which once flourished in
the ancient cities of
Anurādhapura and
Polonnaruwa.

Previous spread: The
Lankatilaka Vihara
stands amid the fertile
highlands a few miles to
the west of Kandy. The
temple was built in the
traditional Sinhalese
style in the fourteenth
century.

51

Dawn at the Ruanweli Dagoba, Anurādhapura. Completed about 90 BC, the 180-foot-high structure was built to cover Buddhist relics.

laity. As a proportion of the total, however, this group has always been relatively insignificant. Today in Sri Lanka there are approximately thirty thousand monks (including novices), of whom less than a thousand are forest dwellers.

The principal occupation of the majority of monks is pastoral care for the ten million lay Buddhists who make up sixty-five per cent of the country's population. This entails preaching religious doctrine, chanting sections of the suttas and generally providing helpful advice. The Sangha once played a leading role in education, but nowadays children go to government schools in which some impecunious monks are employed – in defiance of the Vinaya. As far as the spiritual development of the individual monk is concerned, this is primarily achieved scholastically: meditation is not emphasised at all. Until recently, all full-moon days were set aside for meditation by the laity, but this custom is now rapidly dying out.

Despite a reputation for orthodoxy, largely derived from its association with the Tipitaka, Sinhalese Theravāda Buddhism has in fact long been influenced by extraneous elements of Mahāyāna and Hinduism. In most Buddhist temples there is a shrine to a Hindu god or gods, and while the Buddhist monk does not actually officiate at it, he will not object to a Hindu priest doing so. (Buddhism of course does not deny the existence of gods or spirits, it merely says they cannot help in securing release from the cycle of rebirth.) One particularly conspicuous example of the cohabitation of Sri Lankan Buddhism and Hinduism is the annual Perahera Festival in Kandy, when the images from the town's four chief Hindu temples are paraded alongside the island's most venerated reliquary, believed to contain one of the Buddha's teeth.

In general the boundaries between Mahāyāna and Theravāda Buddhism are not so clear as might reasonably be supposed. Looking at a map of Asia, it would seem logical to conclude that their spheres of influence have always been neatly defined:

Mahāyāna spreading north to China, Tibet and Japan; Theravāda moving south into Sri Lanka, Burma and Thailand. They are often referred to as the Northern and Southern schools. One might further speculate that a cold northern climate encouraged a bookish, sedentary culture, while a warm southern one favoured the pursuit of the ideal of the homeless mendicant. On closer inspection however, this geographical division turns out not to be quite so straightforward. The early Buddhist ideas which today find expression in Theravāda did make a limited impact north of the Himalayas, while Mahāyāna was exported from India to the whole of South-east Asia. As early as the first century BC, a Mahāyāna monastery was founded in Sri Lanka, and in Burma, Mahāyāna had been widely practised before the triumph of Theravāda in the eleventh century. The older tradition therefore did not simply establish itself first and remain unchallenged, rather it had to compete with Mahāyāna for eventual supremacy.

That supremacy was brought about in Burma, not by the religious inclination of the inhabitants, but once again by political circumstances. The boundaries of the countries of South-east Asia were not fixed until comparatively recently and much of the land that is now Burma was for centuries ruled by a people called the Mons who followed the Sri Lankan tradition. The Burmese came originally from the mountains on the border of Eastern Tibet and gradually they migrated down to the fertile plains of the Irrawaddy, founding their capital, Pagan, in AD 849. Initially they combined their animist tribal religion with Mahāyāna Buddhism but, in the eleventh century, the Burmese king, Anawrahta, was converted to Theravāda by a Mon monk. Motivated by deep piety, or so the legend tells us, Anawrahta sent an embassy to the Mon king, requesting a copy of the Tipitaka. Churlishly the king refused, whereupon Anawrahta felt obliged to invade the Mon kingdom and to bring its ruler captive to Pagan. Employing Mon craftsmen and labourers, Pagan was transformed into one of

A cowherd leads his animals through ancient ruins at Anurādhapura. Raids by invading Hindu Tamils obliged the Sinhalese to move the capital to Polonnaruwa in the eighth century.

53

Left: Cyclists pass a traditional temple in Mandalay. Elaborately fashioned corrugated iron and intricately carved timber create a style of architecture which is uniquely Burmese.

Right: The Kuthadaw Pagoda, Mandalay, Burma, where in 1871 the devout King Mindon erected 729 marble tablets engraved with a definitive text of the Burmese Buddhist scriptures.

the great cities of the East, and at the height of its prosperity is said to have contained over 13,000 Buddhist temples and pagodas. Today about 5,000 still remain, in varying stages of ruin, in the dusty fields along the banks of the Irrawaddy. Their present state of disrepair is a consequence of the sacking of the city in the thirteenth century by the Mongol army of Kublai Khan. Despite this calamity the Theravāda Sangha survived, and continued to enjoy the patronage of Burmese kings until the arrival of British colonial government in the nineteenth century.

The relationship between the Burmese Sangha and the state has often been close, particularly under King Mindon, who in 1871 convened the Fifth Buddhist Council in order to carry out a textual revision of the Theravāda scriptures. (Having been verified, these were engraved on 729 large marble tablets, and then erected in Mindon's capital of Mandalay, where they still stand.) For the most part though, the Sangha managed to remain apart from the hurly-burly of everyday politics. It was the dissolution of the monarchy by the British, and the Sangha's consequent loss of royal patronage, which pushed it into an overtly political role. As the embodiment of Burmese cultural identity, Buddhism rapidly became a focus for the nationalist movement. Many monks became involved in agitation against the colonial authorities, and in the crucial stages of the independence struggle in the 1920s and 30s, many were arrested and imprisoned. One, U Wizaya, went on hunger strike after monks were refused permission to wear their robes in gaol, and died in 1929 following

163 days of starvation. Another, U Ottama, was convicted of incitement to rebellion and died in prison in 1939.

The clergy's political activism and outspoken involvement in worldly affairs were not, however, without their Burmese critics. The leader of the nationalist forces at the end of the Second World War, General Aung San, was convinced that complete separation of religious and secular concerns ought once more to be enforced, but his assassination in 1947 ensured that this was never carried out. Instead, after Burma's full independence in 1948, the opposite policy was embarked upon. Buddhism, it was felt, was an ideal accompaniment to Socialism, reinforcing the moral and ethical dimension of a materialist political philosophy. Socialism could also contribute to Buddhism by ensuring that all lay people had equal opportunity to pursue their religion and to progress spiritually. This would, to some extent, help to mitigate the perennial problem of Theravāda societies: that of having the members of the Sangha supported in their religious quest by the mass of the population, whose labour and necessary involvement in the world prevent them personally from advancing along the path to salvation. The culmination of Burmese Buddhist Socialism came in the

Opposite: A marine mechanic on a fifteen-day retreat at a Mandalay monastery. In Burma lay people often join the Sangha for short periods to improve their spiritual understanding.

Previous spread: Pagan, Burma, once one of Asia's most remarkable religious cities. The remains of its 13,000 temples and pagodas have lain in spectacular ruin since the occupation of the city by Kublai Khan in 1287.

elections of 1960, when its chief proponent, U Nu (who had had his ballot boxes painted the colour of the Sangha's robes), campaigned with radical Buddhist social policies, including a commitment to make Buddhism the official state religion, and was overwhelmingly victorious. However, his triumph was short-lived and, after two years of economic disaster, his government was replaced by a military régime.

For the next two decades the military, led by General Ne Win, sought to return to the relationship promoted by successive Burmese kings: limited paternal involvement in the Sangha's affairs, but, in general, a careful separation of church and state. To a degree they were successful; in 1980 the government finally succeeded in creating a centralised system of administration for the Sangha, with which all monks were obliged to register. Nonetheless, during the period of uncertainty which followed Ne Win's resignation in 1988, Buddhist monks once again became active in politics, lending considerable support to those sections of Burmese society in favour of civilian rule and a democratic constitution. To what extent the Sangha will be at the forefront of events in the coming years remains unclear. Certainly, without its acquiescence it will be almost impossible to discover any lasting solution to Burma's political troubles.

Forty years of self-imposed isolation have so far left Burma oblivious to many of the social pressures which have affected other Buddhist countries. It remains locked in a past age (*c*.1950), an age before economic expansion brought consumerism to the ordinary citizen and, throughout the Far East, loosened loyalties to traditional social structures and time-honoured values. Nowhere is the Sangha more widely respected and nowhere is there a greater display of popular piety. There are 124,000 monks in Burma today and it has been estimated that the Burmese layman spends, on average, a quarter of his total income on religious donations. 'To be a Burmese is to be a Buddhist' is an often-quoted proverb and superficially a very apt one. In no other Theravāda country does Buddhism seem such a natural and inevitable part of life. The Sangha is very strong, and the popular religion is ubiquitous. Of course the Theravāda Buddhism of the average Burmese is anything but pure and austere: anthropomorphic images of the Buddha are usually worshipped quite literally, not as

Left: Wooden *nats*, local nature spirits, guard the doorway of a temple in Mandalay.

Right: An evening Dharma class for novices in Botataung, Rangoon. The monastery is maintained by donations from the local community.

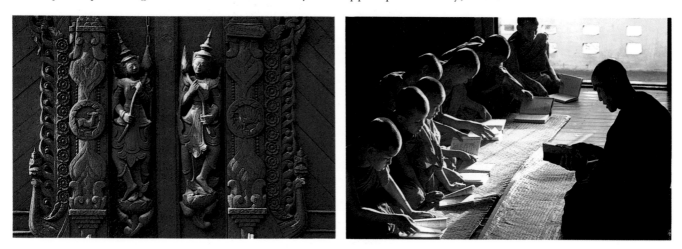

embodiments of a principle; the concept of 'merit' has become debased and is often regarded as a way of ensuring more favourable material circumstances in a future life; and alongside Buddhism there survives (indeed flourishes) superstitious belief in a pantheon of disagreeable spirits, the *nats*, whose behaviour is said to vary from the merely capricious to the diabolically malicious. Despite all of this, Burma is manifestly a country in which the Buddha, the Dhamma and the Sangha are all highly respected. To its credit, the Sangha has not just drifted comfortably along on general

Opposite: Ancient and modern pagodas stand side by side on one of the small islands that dot Inle Lake. The lake lies on the southern Shan Plateau of central Burma.

Wat Mahathat, in the centre of Bangkok, provides a refuge from the cacophony of the city's streets.

Previous spread: Inle Lake, Burma. Novice monks return to their island monastery.

esteem and an ample income. Burmese Theravāda has always stressed the Abhidhamma section of the Tipitaka, particularly those parts concerned with meditation, and, to encourage wider religious awareness, meditation by the laity has been greatly encouraged and simpler forms of practice developed. During the past twenty-five years, one of the few ways that male foreigners have been able to extend their seven-day entry visas, has been to study meditation under an acknowledged master in Rangoon, and many Westerners have taken advantage of this opportunity.

Yet, despite these encouraging trends, the underlying situation remains unstable and the future distinctly uncertain. Since independence Theravāda Buddhism in Burma has escaped having to face up to challenges of the twentieth century. Sooner or later it is going to have to. Just a few hundred miles to the east, in Thailand, the modern age arrived in earnest quite some time ago.

The streets of Bangkok are, as usual, paralysed by traffic, the cacophony of mechanical construction announces the birth of yet another shiny office tower, and on every street corner lurid billboards importune the harassed pedestrian. Nonetheless, among the fumes and the rush-hour crowds, the shaven heads of Buddhist monks can still be glimpsed, seemingly aloof from the urban mayhem. It would be hard to imagine a scene of greater incongruity.

Never having been invaded and colonised, the Thais see nothing intrinsically threatening about Western culture and its associated technological paraphernalia. Development and material progress have long been welcomed and their effect on the indigenous way of life does not seem to have been seriously questioned. For the Thais, the game of modern life is there to be played and won and, unlike the Burmese, they have never for a moment considered refusing to take part. And yet, despite the discothèques, the blue jeans and the shopping malls, there are still 340,000 monks in Thailand and over half of the male population has spent some time in one of the

country's 28,000 monasteries. Every summer monsoon, about a quarter of a million Thai men go on a Rains Retreat and become temporarily affiliated to the Sangha. This kind of paradox makes Thailand arguably the most fascinating of Theravāda countries today. Buddhism is struggling hard to find a new role in a dynamic society and is both suffering setbacks and making progress.

Like the Burmese, the Thais conquered the territory they now occupy. Originally from southern China, they too moved down from the hills into a fertile plain, where a wide, sluggish river flooded the rice paddies that fed the growing population. Like the Burmese, as they expanded southwards, the Thais came under the cultural influence of the Mons who were Theravāda Buddhists. Initially they were subject to the Khmer people (from what is now Cambodia), but about 1260 they managed to throw off Khmer domination and to found the Kingdom of Sukhothai, the forerunner of the modern Thai state. At the beginning of the fourteenth century the King invited monks from Sri Lanka to reorganise the Sangha and to instruct its members in Pāli sacred literature. As a result Thailand inherited the Sinhalese system of state control and, instead of the Sangha being sustained as an independent order of religious contemplatives, it became a national institution under the direct supervision of the Crown.

Despite the inappropriateness of this arrangement in terms of strict Theravāda idealism, the Thai monarchy's involvement with the Sangha has been surprisingly constructive. Various rulers have initiated reforms and caused collections of the scriptures to be made, the most notable of these royal patrons being King Mongkut, who was himself a monk for twenty-seven years prior to his coronation in 1851. While a member of the Sangha, King Mongkut initiated a reform movement, the *Dhammayuttika-Nikāya*, which insisted on a stricter discipline than that practised by the majority, or *Mahānikāya*. These two groups still make up the Thai Sangha today

Sealed in polythene to preserve their shine, modern Buddha images wait for buyers at a Bangkok street market.

63

Opposite: Hand of the colossal seated Buddha at Wat Si Chum, Sukhothai, onto which layers of gold leaf have been pressed by generations of worshippers. The Buddha is in the posture of Bhumisparsa, in which he touches the earth to call it to witness his victory over Māra, the force of evil.

Previous spread: Evening falls on the ruins of Wat Chetuphon, Sukhothai, Thailand. Sukhothai was the capital of a Thai Buddhist kingdom from the mid-thirteenth to the mid-fifteenth century.

and loosely speaking the distinction between them is that the reformed sect pays more attention to personal spirituality and meditation than does the Mahānikāya, which is chiefly concerned with pastoral care for the laity.

However beneficial King Mongkut's reforms may have been, once he came to the throne, the connection between the Crown and the Sangha inevitably became closer than ever before. This relationship was given practical expression after his death in the first Administration of the Buddhist Order Act of 1902, under the terms of which the Sangha was organised as a branch of the Thai civil service, the senior official being the Supreme Patriarch, appointed personally by the King. Subordinate to the Supreme Patriarch, it was decided there should be a Council of Elders and (in descending order of importance) Ecclesiastical Regional Heads, Provincial Heads, District Heads, Sub-District Heads and, finally, the Abbots of the various monasteries. This system has remained in force to the present day.

Of course the existence of an elaborate bureaucracy does not necessarily affect the individual monk's strict adherence to the Vinaya discipline, but in practice it does have consequences. One of the religious authorities' primary functions is organising a series of examinations for which monks are required to study. Although it is desirable that monks should be literate and studious, it is less obviously beneficial for spiritual accomplishment to be reduced to a formula. The personal quest for Enlightenment becomes little more than the pursuit of a higher diploma. Allied to this very worldly notion of achievement is the exploitation of the Sangha for the sake of social advancement. Ambitious young men from economically poor or deprived backgrounds sometimes join a monastery knowing that, if they gain conspicuous qualifications, employment may be open to them in areas of Thai society for which they would never otherwise have been considered. Similarly, more complex areas of study may require the monk to attend one of Bangkok's Buddhist universities, in which case the excitement of life in the city is added to the advantages of social mobility.

One positive side effect of Thailand's colossal religious bureaucracy is the ease with which large sections of the male population can spend short periods of their lives in a monastery. There is just a standard form to be completed, issued by the Department of Religion in Bangkok. The practice of young men spending a few weeks as a monk, usually during the summer rains, was initiated by the royal family and the present King of Thailand had his head shaved as a young man and spent some weeks as a bhikkhu, begging for his daily food in the traditional manner. Any man is eligible to join the Sangha, either temporarily or permanently. Those who become ordained for long periods are generally either in their early twenties, or else late in life, seeking refuge from the world after decades of work and responsibility.

Having allowed itself to become a national church, the Sangha is now an integral part of Thailand's establishment. This may make it very secure politically and financially, but it does not guarantee it public esteem, or make it an organisation especially well suited to a rapidly changing society. Its strongholds are in the relatively undeveloped Thai countryside, where the relationship between monks and villagers, matured over centuries, can carry on undisturbed. There the bhikkhus still leave the monastery in the early morning and go out on their alms round. They are still treated with great respect and their way of life acknowledged to be superior to that of the world. As long as they are seen to keep to the fundamentals of the Vinaya – chastity, poverty, temperance and so on – food will be provided for them, new living quarters constructed, and the temple buildings repaired. All such donations provide opportunities for the laity to acquire merit; to improve their karma. For their part, the monks will attend important local events and conduct 'merit-making' ceremonies

A novice forest monk
meditating beneath a
mosquito net at Wat
Parelai, Ban Chiang,
north-east Thailand.

Opposite: Characteristic
bell-shaped stupa,
Sukhothai, central
Thailand.

The monks of Wat Parelai eat their morning meal. All the food is donated by the villagers of Ban Chiang.

Previous spread: Monks returning from their early morning alms round to the forest monastery of Wat Parelai, Ban Chiang.

when called upon to do so. The texts for these will have been memorised and are generally taken from the Sutta-pitaka. In general, such monks give little thought to the sublimities of their religion. The attainment of Nirvāna is widely thought to be a hopelessly unrealistic ambition, and meditation is seldom practised. Apart from desultory study of the Tipitaka, they devote themselves to being a benevolent and harmonious influence in society.

Not even deep in the countryside however has the status quo remained entirely unaffected by modern times. There are now state schools and the Sangha has lost its monopoly of education. Whereas previously bhikkhus were regarded as the most learned members of the community, this adjunct to the dignity of their simple life has now largely disappeared. It is a change compounded by the departure of many of the more academically able monks to the city, in pursuit of higher education.

In expanding urban areas, particularly Bangkok, the traditional role of the monk is almost impossible to sustain. For example, it is very difficult for them to go on a morning alms round and many city temples now manage their own funds. The mutually beneficial relationship which can exist between monastery and laity in a small, stable agricultural community is scarcely possible in the teeming and unruly streets of a metropolis with five million inhabitants. The monks are often as ignorant of their neighbours as the average city dweller, and this can have unforeseen consequences. Generally it is the lay people who insist on the monks' rigid adherence to the Vinaya discipline and as the monastery is dependent on them for its very existence, the monks have little alternative but to comply. This restraint disappears as soon as the monastery controls its own budget. Nowadays it is not difficult to encounter a good deal of cynicism about the behaviour of some members of the Sangha. In the words of a leading Thai Buddhist academic, referring to one of Bangkok's larger monasteries, 'Just about anything goes on in there. Instead of

leading the people spiritually, they merely follow the fashions of the modern world.'

There have been various attempts to make the Sangha more responsive to the needs of late twentieth-century society. Chief, and most controversial, among these has been the training of monks to take part in community development projects. While much of practical value has been achieved – roads laid, wells dug and schools built – this kind of work is so obviously at odds with the traditional Theravāda view of the monk's role that there has been vociferous opposition. There is also the danger that as soon as the Sangha becomes directly involved in government spending programmes, it has entered into areas liable to prove politically contentious.

To understand just how intractable some of the Sangha's problems are, one has only to consider the dilemma posed by the recent, and continuing, enlargement of women's role in Thai society. For two and a half thousand years, the history of Theravāda Buddhism has been almost exclusively male. Notable female Buddhists have been conspicuous chiefly by their absence. Ananda, the Buddha's cousin and disciple, is said to have asked three times for women to be admitted to the Order and it was only with considerable reluctance that the Buddha eventually agreed. The cause of the Buddha's hesitation has been much disputed, some claiming that it was because the life of a religious mendicant left a woman vulnerable to abuse and attack, while others more straightforwardly insist it was because he feared women would undermine the moral determination of the monks. History has conspired with social orthodoxy and the latter view prevails, so much so that in Theravāda countries women are generally regarded as the greatest of all impediments to a man's spiritual progress. In Thailand today there are special places reserved for monks on buses and trains so that they do not run the risk of being obliged to sit next to a woman.

The female ordination lineage died out everywhere in the Theravāda Buddhist world as long ago as AD 456. It is therefore impossible for a woman to join an

With their studies and simple living conditions, the forest monks of Wat Parelai follow the teaching of the Buddha.

73

established religious community. Despite the demands of educated Thai women for equality in religion as in other aspects of life, there is very little the Thai Sangha can do to oblige. Their predicament is a revealing example of Theravāda history and contemporary Thailand being unwittingly, and perhaps insolubly, at loggerheads.

Despite the numerous problems faced by the Buddhist establishment, there are more encouraging counter-currents. It is even possible that Thailand could eventually become the centre of a Theravāda revival. Monks in increasing numbers are leaving the official monastic structure to travel to remote areas of the country where they live in simple conditions, spending a large part of their time practising meditation. Until very recently, those who refused to conform to accepted patterns of behaviour were regarded with extreme disfavour. Even leaving the monastery to go on pilgrimage was thought irresponsible and anti-social. The Buddhist ideal of ancient India, the wandering religious mendicant, was held in very low esteem. One man, more than any other, has been responsible for the transformation.

Bhikkhu Buddhadāsa is widely regarded as the greatest Theravāda thinker and scholar of the present age yet, for the past twenty-five years, most of his energies have been spent on the establishment of a forest hermitage, Suan Mokh, near the obscure town of Chaiya in southern Thailand. At first no more than a few huts among the trees, the monastery now has a lecture hall, a museum, and a library. Its ideals however, have not changed and the monks still sit in meditation outside, shaded perhaps by a parasol, but completely unencumbered by the accoutrements of organised religion. Buddhadāsa is in the best sense a religious fundamentalist. He has translated the Tipitaka from Pāli into the vernacular and, risking the wrath of the establishment, advocated that the laity should read it without the standard commentaries. He has also been outspokenly critical of those developments in Theravāda which he considers alien, extraneous, or even antithetical to the teachings and intentions of the Buddha himself. The trend for monks to become involved in social work has consistently met with his stern disapproval. Rather he has urged his followers to begin again on the difficult path of spiritual self-discovery, through respect for the Vinaya, and diligent meditation. Now over eighty years old, Buddhadāsa has lived to see his work become a remarkable success. Not only are there thousands of visitors to Suan Mokh every year there are today many other Buddhist centres in Thailand motivated by a similar idealism. For example, one of the country's most respected meditation masters, Ajahn Chah, has established more than twenty remote forest monasteries. Particularly encouraging is the fact that educated, urban dwellers who had little interest in established Buddhism, are among those most attracted to this revival of Theravāda purity.

The twenty-five years of Buddhadāsa's experiment are of course insignificant when compared with the two thousand five hundred years since the Buddha's Enlightenment. It is nonetheless tempting to see history turning full circle. For two millennia, throughout South-east Asia, Theravāda Buddhism became ever more involved in the apparatus of the state, further and further removed from the noble and austere ideals of the early Indian religion. Unfortunately, in times of sweeping and fundamental social change, being a pillar of the established order is not necessarily an advantage. As Theravāda Buddhism looks to the twenty-first century, it may well find that hope for an otherwise uncertain future lies in a return to the first principles of its long tradition – to the words of the Buddha himself and to the simple and meditative way of life that is the substance of his religion.

Opposite: The great Thai Buddhist reformer, Bhikkhu Buddhadasa, at his retreat centre, Suan Mokh, in southern Thailand.

Following spread: The hands of a monk meditating in the shade of the forest at Wat Parelai, Ban Chiang.

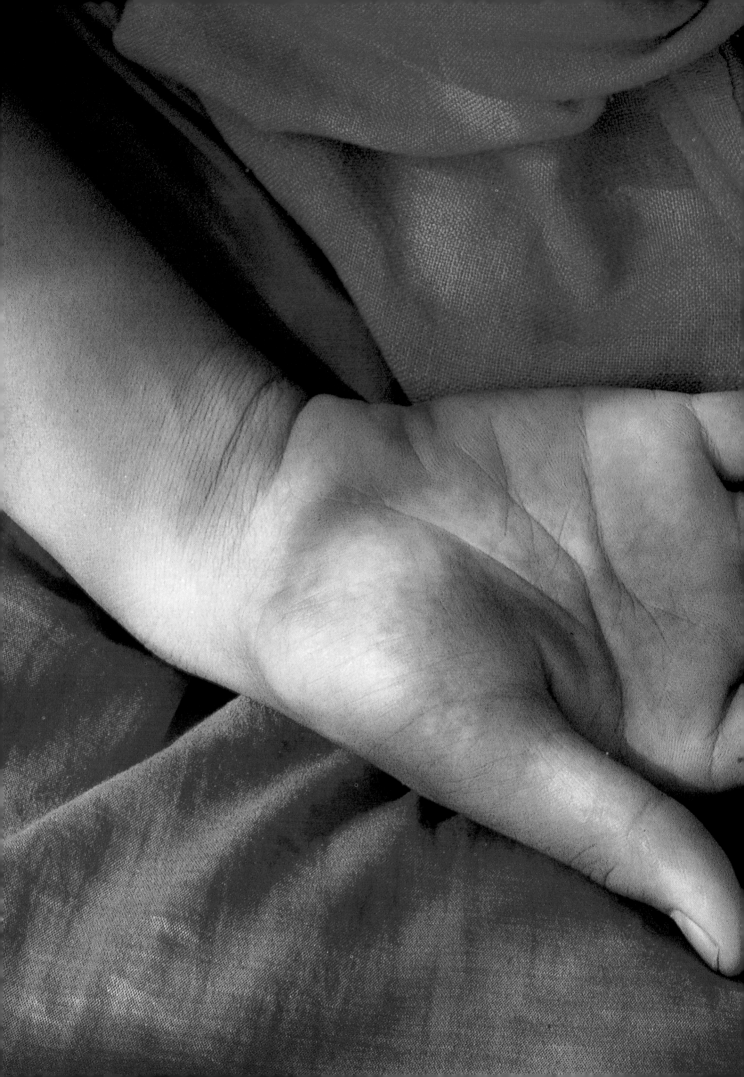

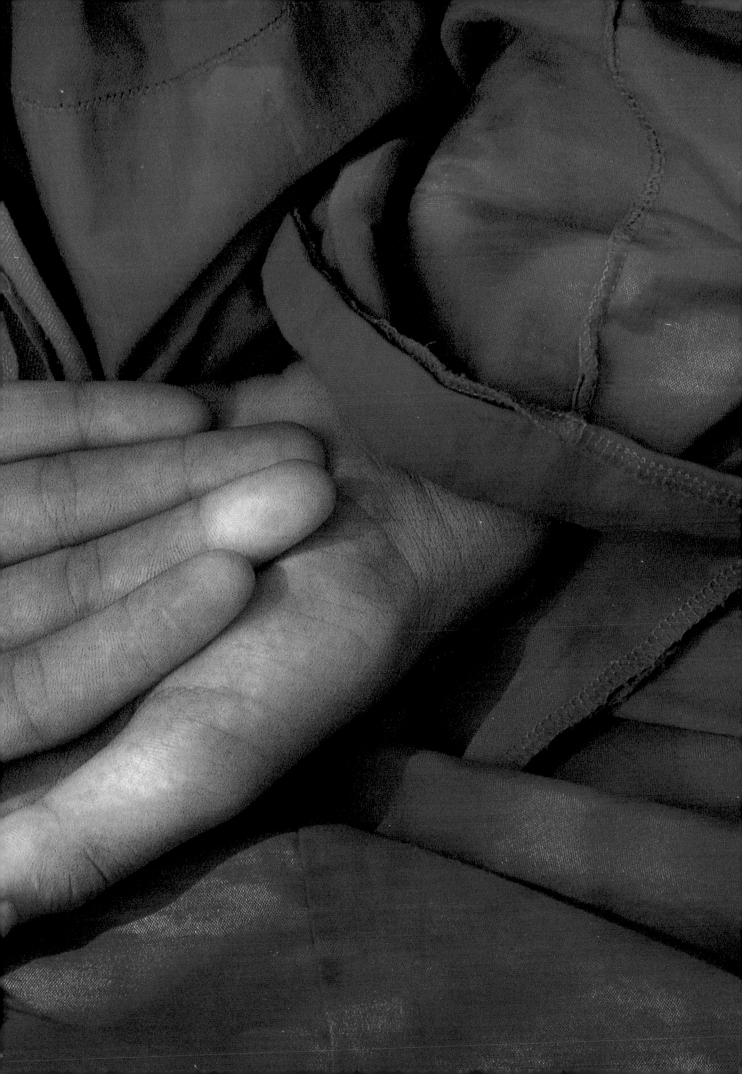

The Buddha Mind

3

Japanese paths to Enlightenment

'Although the Buddha had great wisdom at birth, he sat in training for six years; although Bodhidharma transmitted the Buddha-mind, we still hear the echoes of his nine years facing a wall.'

Dōgen, *Rules for Meditation*

Three thousand feet up in the mountains of central Japan stand the venerable wooden buildings of the seven-hundred-year-old monastery of Eiheiji. At half past four, the clangour of the day's first bell fractures the silence of the *zendō*. There the monks lie asleep, each man identifiable only as a hump on a bench beneath a quilt. After just a few seconds of stirring and stretching, they begin to file out to wash. As they pass, the bell-ringer, a novice, bows deeply to each shambling figure in turn.

In Zen monasteries, the zendō's most important function is as the meditation hall, but it serves also as both dormitory and refectory. The primacy of meditation, or *zāzen*, in the lives of their inhabitants is thereby continually underlined. Each morning, a monk wakes to an immediate and inescapable reminder of the chief preoccupation of his existence. The section (six feet by three) of the platform on which he sleeps, eats and meditates, is literally his home. Eiheiji is the head temple of the Sōtō Zen school. No other Buddhist order places greater emphasis on meditation. The word 'Zen' itself means, in essence, 'meditation'.

The first formal zāzen session begins at a quarter to five, as the monks, now solemn and dignified in ankle-length black ropes, file back into the zendō, going to their allotted places on the *tan*, the wide bench running around the room, covered in tatami matting. Each monk has a round black cushion, eighteen inches in diameter, called a *zafu*, on which he sits, straight-backed and cross-legged, facing the wall.

'Meditation' can be a confusing word as there are many different sorts of mental exercise employed by the various Buddhist schools. In Sōtō Zen, the technique may be described as 'Serene Reflection'. The practitioner settles himself on the zafu by briefly swaying his body from side to side, and places his left hand on the palm of his right with the ends of the thumbs touching. Then putting the tip of his tongue at the back of his top front teeth, he inhales and exhales sharply several times before adopting a normal, relaxed rate of breathing. Keeping his eyes open, he tries neither to think nor not to think – indeed he tries not to try. 'Just sitting' is a phrase often employed to indicate the simplicity and purity of this procedure. The theory of this passive and apparently simplistic technique is that profound religious awareness already exists within the mind. The fundamental necessity is to calm the distracting clutter of everyday consciousness so that what has always been there, but unwittingly ignored, can now be experienced.

After forty-five minutes, a gong sounds and the monks carefully, and in ritual order, slide from their cushions, plump them up for use later in the day and then proceed to

Opposite: Carrying food in the prescribed manner, a novice runs along one of the covered walkways at the Sōtō Zen Monastery of Eiheiji, Japan. In the Sōtō tradition all life's activities, however mundane, must be undertaken in a religious spirit.

the main hall of the monastery for the morning service. At the arrival of the Abbot the ceremony begins to the pulse of a muffled drum, a single chant soon swelling to a low chorus. The Heart Sūtra is being recited, the most concise statement of the nature of Ultimate Wisdom in the whole of Mahāyāna Buddhist philosophy. After an hour of chanting, prayers and prostrations, the daily ritual comes to an end and silent, with heads lowered, the monks return to the zendō for breakfast. It is 6.30 am. The life of a Sōtō Zen monk is extremely demanding, and not just because of the uncomfortable routine and the strict discipline. Sōtō Zen maintains that any distinction between religious activity – meditation, prayer – and secular activity – eating, washing – is entirely false. Pursuing the Buddhist path to Enlightenment, it insists, requires all of life's activities to be undertaken with the mind of meditation. It is absolutely no use trying to develop religious awareness in formal periods of zāzen, only to lapse into worldly inattention while drinking a bowl of soup. The commitment of the Zen monk to the religious life is therefore absolute and every aspect of his existence is formalised to promote this unremitting concentration. Of course it is intended that such concentration should eventually become completely natural, so that constant effort is no longer required. Calm control must be substituted for the anarchy of everyday consciousness. When this has been achieved it is quite possible to eat a sandwich or read a newspaper with a mind focused and serene.

Left: Zazen, Serene Reflection Meditation.

Right: Cross-legged on tatami matting, the monks of Eiheiji attend the morning service in the main hall of the monastery.

At Eiheiji, breakfast is followed by a period of vigorous manual labour. In most Buddhist traditions, monks do little physical work. From the very beginning of the religion, it was considered unsuitable for them to engage in agriculture because of the harm they might bring to insects and small animals. The Zen schools have long taken a different view; in the eighth century the Zen master Hyakujyo Nehan famously remarked 'No work, no food'.

Constructed on different levels up and down the mountainside, Eiheiji is held together by a grid of long, steep staircases. These are made, like virtually everything else, from magnificent planks of cedar wood. Half-running, half-stumbling down dozens of steps, bare feet searching for a grip on boards awash with days of rain, comes a troop of novices with brooms and pails. Very soon the corridors are choked with figures on their hands and knees scrubbing, polishing and splashing in the wet. Under the vociferous supervision of a senior monk they run backwards and forwards on all fours, pushing cleaning cloths before them. Yelled at, sodden, gasping for breath, they fall over, pick themselves up, and struggle on with desperate determination.

Two weeks earlier, these novices had stood patiently for hours, waiting to be admitted through Eiheiji's imposing main gate. Now, accepted into the monastery, it

Opposite: A Sōtō Zen novice from Eiheiji dressed to go on pilgrimage. In the travelling pack he carries on his chest are his eating utensils, important passages from Dōgen's *Shobogenzo* and a letter of recommendation from his abbot.

The Buddha Mind

Left: Monks taking breakfast at Eiheiji. In the Sōtō tradition all aspects of daily life are ritualised and thereby given religious significance.

Right: Dawn at Eiheiji on a wet morning in early March.

will be a year, perhaps longer, before they are allowed to set foot off the premises. To begin with not even letters from relatives will successfully penetrate their isolation. Their lives will be physically hard, dominated by an unrelenting routine, their individuality rapidly being subordinated to the insistent demands of gongs and bells.

Eiheiji is a training monastery and, out of its 150 monks, only 30 are fully ordained. The majority of the remaining 120 will eventually become priests in one or other of the 15,000 Sōtō Zen temples throughout Japan. Eiheiji is therefore more a seminary than a monastery in the commonly understood sense. However, a crucial difference exists between its monks and their counterparts training for pastoral responsibility in, say, the Christian church. Many of them are there not because of a sense of religious vocation. They will become priests because their fathers were priests before them (marriage is widespread throughout Japanese Buddhist orders) and the maintenance of a temple has become a hereditary occupation. Of all the Buddhist sects in Japan, Sōtō Zen is arguably the most disestablished – Eiheiji itself was deliberately founded in a remote mountain region to be far away from the machinations of the court at Kyoto – and yet despite this stated preference for meditative solitude, it, like every other Japanese Buddhist school, has been bound into the structure of Japanese society. While Sōtō Zen has produced more than its fair share of remarkable men and indeed its founder, Dōgen, is often claimed to be the greatest figure in Japanese religious history, among the lower ranks of its organisation the priesthood is regarded as a job – no more and no less. In consequence the severity of the discipline at Eiheiji may be seen partly as an attempt to instil some instinct for religious fundamentals into those who would otherwise have little inclination towards the spiritual life.

Opposite: A novice, required to run when moving about the monastery, dashes along a polished corridor at Eiheiji. Vigorous physical exertion is an integral part of the Zen training.

Most of the trainees are in their twenties and, as many have come from the chief Sōtō Zen academic institution, Komazawa University in Tokyo, they already have a detailed understanding of Buddhist history and philosophy. Eiheiji however has a practical rather than a scholastic atmosphere, mainly because of the number of pilgrims who come to visit the temple each year. Sōtō is the largest of the two principal Zen sects in Japan, having about seven million adherents. The country's present population is approximately 120 million so this is a small though scarcely negligible proportion. To cope with the thousands of visitors, a new reception centre has been attached to the old monastery and there pilgrims may stay for up to a week, receiving instruction and practising their meditation. The monastery exhibits a good deal of paternal concern for the spiritual well-being of its congregation and large numbers of monks are kept busy shepherding new arrivals and escorting them to those areas of the ancient buildings to which, at certain times of the day, they are permitted access.

82

The Imperial Gate at Eiheiji flanked by 600 year old cedar trees.

Other monks at Eiheiji work on a Sōtō Zen newspaper, distributed throughout the country. Yet despite the money spent and the effort expended on the promotion of a relationship between monastery and laity, it is not difficult to encounter voices of cynicism. 'Japanese people work so hard they have no time for meditation', is a frequent comment, often followed by the rueful observation that 'People only expect priests to conduct ceremonies and to preside over rites for the dead'. Even at Eiheiji, a remarkable and thriving religious institution, it is possible to hear such echoes of the debate which has preoccupied Japanese Buddhists since the end of the Second World War: has Buddhism become detached from the sources of its inspiration? Has it become a religion only of forms and observances? Is Buddhism in Japan slowly dying?

Fortunately, most of the time at Eiheiji such dire speculations seem beside the point. There is anyway seldom the time for them. The monks have four or more zāzen sessions a day and these can be up to two hours in length. Punctuating the otherwise implacable routine are two occasions each month when individuals may ask the Abbot questions about their spiritual progress and six mornings when they are given sufficient free time to wash their clothes and have their heads shaved. Such has been the pattern of life since the thirteenth century, when its details and observances were first laid down by Dōgen, in his great work the *Shōbōgenzō*, or 'Eye of the True Law'.

One thousand, seven hundred years before the foundation of Eiheiji, the historical Buddha Shākyamuni sat with his followers in very different surroundings in the northern Indian plains. For no apparent reason, to illustrate no argument, the Buddha suddenly held up a flower and looked at it. Of his disciples only one,

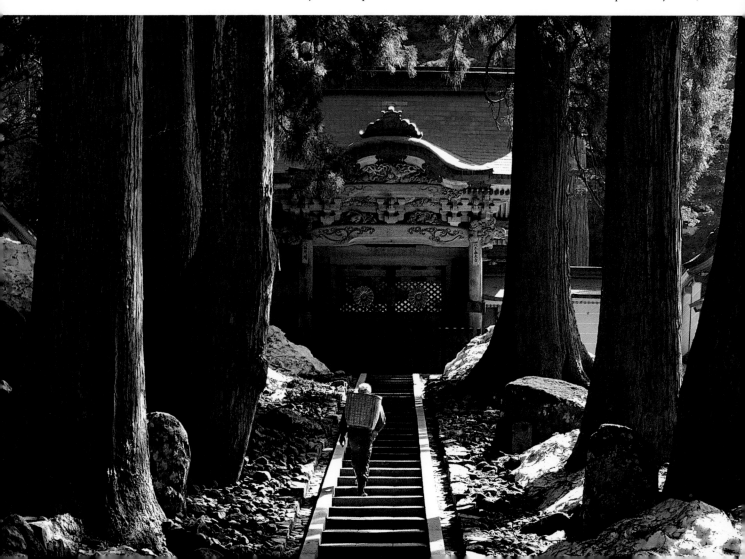

Mahākāshyapa, saw any importance in this gesture and he made no comment, asked no question, only smiled. Such a trivial episode might seem scarcely worth History's trouble to record, yet for Zen Buddhists this incident is of the greatest significance.

The central purpose of Zen is the awakening of indescribable illumination and it is the single-mindedness with which it pursues this goal that separates it from other Buddhist schools. Followers of Zen certainly do not question the fundamentals of the Buddha's teaching, they merely insist that as Enlightenment is attainable, it must be immediately and directly pursued. Although the Buddha's rules for rational and virtuous behaviour provide an essential preliminary to meditation by clearing the mind of vice and unreason, it is the very *fact* of his Enlightenment which is the crucial part of his message. Thus, the Buddha's teachings about the nature of physical reality and the human mind are of incalculable value, but nonetheless ultimately subordinate to his demonstration that life contains the potential for transcendent experience.

But what of Mahākāshyapa and the flower? This episode, the Zen tradition maintains, is the first illustration that fundamental to Buddhism is a transmission of Wisdom beyond the capabilities of language. The Buddha, in his enlightened state, looked at the flower and perceived its true Reality, a vision uncorrupted by the limitations of the senses, or habits and prejudices of the mind. His attention unexpectedly drawn to the flower, Mahākāshyapa suddenly saw as the Buddha saw and he too became enlightened. This experience is known in Zen as *satori* and, far from being random or haphazard, it is the product of intense and prolonged meditation. Mahākāshyapa silently received a teaching that would have been

Inscription under the eaves of Eiheiji. Although the monastery was founded in the thirteenth century, most of its wooden buildings have been reconstructed during the last two hundred years due to fire damage.

For a few quiet moments a young visitor contemplates the raked gravel of the famous Zen garden of Daisen-in, at the Rinzai Zen Monastery of Daitokuji in Kyoto.

Previous spread: A novice scrubs Eiheiji's wooden floors in the raw cold and semi-darkness of a late winter morning. Cleaning is said to wipe away delusion.

impossible by rational, philosophical methods and, in so doing, achieved the primary objective of Zen Buddhism – the realisation by the religious practitioner of the Buddha-mind of Enlightenment. It is this quest which for the devout Zen Buddhist is the substance of life.

An entire millennium passed before, in AD 520, the eminent Indian Buddhist scholar, Bodhidharma, arrived in the Chinese city of Nanking. This was not in itself a particularly remarkable occurrence as China had been subject to Buddhist influence since the first century AD. The Emperor Wu-ti received his distinguished visitor courteously and, knowing him to be a highly regarded religious authority, asked him to define for him the fundamental principle of Buddhism. The Emperor is said to have shown considerable Imperial dissatisfaction with the answer which he promptly received, namely 'Vast Emptiness'. Without elaborating, the scholar left the court and went to live in a mountain cave. There he meditated for nine years facing a wall of rock, resolutely refusing to speak to any of his many visitors.

Bodhidharma has another claim to fame besides that of being the man who subsequently introduced Ch'an (in Japanese, 'Zen') Buddhism to China. In the Zen tradition he is the twenty-eighth link in an unbroken chain of spiritual transmission from master to pupil extending back to Mahākāshyapa, and consequently to the Buddha himself. It is this chain which supports the Zen assertion that their approach is the purest to be found among any of the Buddhist sects in the world today.

Relinquishing his cave, Bodhidharma, by now rather more inclined to loquacity, famously summarised his message in the following verse:

A special transmission outside the scriptures;
No dependence on words and letters;
Direct pointing to the soul of man;
Seeing into one's own nature and attainment of Buddhahood.

These four simple lines make plain the fact that Zen is essentially a practical religion in which the emphasis is not on disputation and analysis, but on actual achievement brought about by personal effort. It is anti-intellectual, claiming that the highest realms of Buddhist philosophy will not, of themselves, lead anyone to Enlightenment. Paradoxically these apparently iconoclastic ideas stem from an understanding and acceptance of the conclusions of classic Indian Mahāyāna thought. Bodhidharma's insistence that the essence of Buddhism is 'Vast Emptiness', is far from being a deliberately obscure and provocative remark. The immensely influential Indian Mādhyamika school of philosophy has argued that essential nature of all things is a mystical 'emptiness'. It claimed that Reality is concealed from us by our own ignorance and our insistence on trying to approach the Ultimate and Absolute from within the limiting framework of conceptual thought and language. Through deep meditation we come to see that what we term 'empty' or 'void' is in fact the nature of the All. It is with the practical business of gaining this awareness that Zen Buddhism is solely concerned.

Bodhidharma was the first of six Chinese Ch'an (Zen) patriarchs. The sixth, Hui-neng, appointed no successor and the religion, carried on by his disciples, evolved into five principal schools. Despite this schism and the severing of the line of direct transmission from Mahākāshyapa, Ch'an rapidly gained in popularity until eventually it became the main (but by no means the only) form of Buddhism in China. Of the five Ch'an sects, two came to be predominant: Lin-Chi and Tsao-tung. In Japan these were later known as Rinzai and Sōtō.

To those unfamiliar with the cultural history of the East, Zen may appear to be a peculiarly Japanese form of Buddhism. Yet in fact its methods are Chinese in origin, and both its philosophical background and its claims to a unique legitimacy are derived from India. The history of Zen in Japan begins with scholars returning

The hands of Daibutsu, or 'Great Buddha' at Kamakura. The 37ft high bronze statue of the Buddha Amida was cast in 1252.

89

footsore and possibly seasick from China, loaded down with boxes of sutras and commentaries. What is true of Zen is also true of the other Buddhist sects which took root in Japanese soil: they are all of Chinese inspiration. Zen, however, played a special part in this process because it was one of the products of the Chinese mind which the Japanese took most to heart and which therefore became central to much that is remarkable and original in their civilisation.

Kyoto, capital of Japan from 794 until 1868, is virtually synonymous with Japanese culture, and Myōshin-ji, to the north-west of the city, is one of the greatest of all Rinzai Zen monasteries. As one strolls along its gravel paths between the wooden temples, the noise of the city quickly recedes and a healing atmosphere of calm descends. Behind an unassuming gateway and a tall screen of clipped box hedges is set out the famous sixteenth-century garden of Taizōin. There, sitting in the tea pavilion or among the restless fronds of the bamboo grove, listening to the splash of a waterfall or watching the carp indolently circling the pond, one is swiftly soothed and absorbed by a mood of tranquil introspection.

Left: The eighth-century Buddha in the cave temple of Sŏkkuram, South Korea. This white granite image shows the Buddha 'Calling the Earth to Witness', and is considered to be one of the greatest masterpieces of Buddhist art.

Right: Rice planting at sunset near Kyongju, south-east Korea. The Sŏkkuram Buddha nearby was carved during the heyday of this ancient city.

Rinzai was introduced to Japan from China in 1191 by a monk, Eisai. At first the new religion was greeted by a distinct lack of enthusiasm in Kyoto, but further north in Kamakura, not far from present-day Tokyo, it provoked a far more appreciative reaction. From 1192 until 1868, Kamakura was effectively a second Japanese capital, being the seat of power of the Shoguns, a line of military dictators who ruled the country in tandem with the Emperor. The Rinzai, or 'Sudden School', method of seeking Enlightenment appealed greatly to military minds and certainly more than the gentler, gradual Sōtō approach. Today Rinzai is still known as 'Warrior Zen' and Sōtō, somewhat dismissively, as 'Farmer Zen'. However, despite centuries of patronage by Japan's military hierarchy and aristocracy, Sōtō remains the larger of two Japanese sects. It is difficult to say which of the two has had the greater effect on Japanese life and culture. In the West it is generally supposed that Rinzai has been much more influential, but this may be partly because Dr Daisetz T. Suzuki, the scholar who more than any other introduced Zen to the English-speaking world, was a follower of the Rinzai school.

Among the cherry trees and chrysanthemums of Myōshin-ji, it is sometimes difficult to conceive of the connection between such a supremely civilised landscape and a caste of military authoritarians. The basis for such a relationship lies in the principal distinction between the Rinzai and Sōtō schools: the use of the *kōan*. Both Rinzai and Sōtō would agree that the object of religious practice is the realisation of the Buddha-mind. Sōtō maintains that the way to achieve this realisation is through

Opposite: A monk holds one of the 81,137 wooden printing blocks preserved in the library at Hae'in-sa Temple, South Korea. They form one of the most complete collections of Buddhist scriptures in the world.

At the monastery of Hwaŏm-Sa, South Korea, a monk walks along the sunlit pathway leading to one of the outlying buildings.

Opposite: Hae'in-sa in the rugged forest scenery of the Kaya-san National Park, South Korea.

The Buddha Mind

Left: The Horyuji Temple complex at Nara, Japan, contains some of the oldest wooden buildings in the world. It was opened in AD 607 by Prince Shotoku, the man sometimes referred to as the father of Japanese Buddhism.

Right: Water-lilies in a pool in Kyoto; a setting for calm reflection.

zazen, transforming the whole of life into continuous meditation and thereby endeavouring to live as the Buddha himself lived in his Enlightened state. The Rinzai school on the other hand insists that Enlightenment may be prompted by meditation on a kōan, a short question or statement which is in itself illogical, but which can hold the attention of the intellect allowing a higher faculty to suddenly take over. Perhaps the most famous of these is 'What is the sound of one hand clapping?', but there are around 1,700 others, of which perhaps 700 are in frequent use.

In the Rinzai tradition the relationship between the Zen master and his pupil is of immense importance and during private interviews the master gives to his pupil a kōan which he deems suitable for his particular spiritual condition. The precise details of what is said and what occurs are always kept strictly secret, but teaching methods can certainly be rather abrupt. Rinzai Zen argues that to have any hope of perceiving the Truth we must be jolted out of our habitual modes of thought and if physical violence can be of some use in this respect, then so be it.

It is this obedience and commitment, combined with the arduous pursuit of a very elusive objective, which presumably recommended Rinzai Zen to the military. It is however, extremely important not to jump to superficial conclusions. Zen has brought to the apparently secular arts of swordsmanship, archery and judo an astonishing degree of aesthetic and spiritual refinement. Archery, for example is practised in Japan as a form of meditation, the underlying theory being that it is possible to achieve a level of co-ordination between mind and body so perfect, that the customary dualism ceases to have any real meaning. Hitting the target, in the literal sense, is not of the least importance.

Opposite: The serene face of the Bodhisattva Miroku, a seventh-century wooden image in the Chuguji Convent, Nara. Miroku is contemplating how to achieve the salvation of mankind.

Previous spread: A Kegon monk practices Zen meditation near the Hwaŏm-Sa Temple, South Korea. Buddhism originally came to Japan from Korea.

96

Ten minutes' walk up a quiet suburban road from Myōshin-ji, beside a large lake generously scattered with wildfowl, is the small Rinzai temple of Ryōanji. The buildings themselves are on a modest scale, half lost in vegetation, but it is not the architecture which has been responsible for Ryōanji's international fame. Surrounded on three sides by an old earthen wall and on the fourth by a creaking wooden verandah, is a rectangle of white, raked sand and fifteen rocks split into five groups. This classically austere arrangement is the most famous of all Zen gardens. Although differing theories of the relationship between man and nature have been worked out in the gardens of Italian palazzi, French châteaux and English country houses, nowhere in the world has the art of gardening been invested with the same degree of religious and philosophical intensity as it has in Japan. Ryōanji is much more than just an abstract composition: it is a subject intended for meditation. This garden, unlike most others, is unchanging. There are no flowers to fade and no leaves to fall.

The only changes which can occur among the inert forms of sand and stone will be induced by the mind and perception of the onlooker.

Earlier this century, Ryōanji fell into disrepair; the sand went unraked and the walls began to crack and crumble. It was a thing of the past. Nowadays, happily, it is pristine once more and regarded as a great national treasure. This doubtless reflects Japan's new spirit of confidence and self-respect, but it may also be true that this revival of concern has been generated partly by outside interest. There is good reason to believe that foreign, especially American, fascination with Zen has spurred the Japanese to a greater appreciation of some aspects of their own culture. Unfortunately this has a regrettable side effect. Anyone wishing to meditate at Ryōanji today is likely to have to compete with busloads of Japanese schoolchildren and tourists. One is left to reflect ruefully that just as Westerners now wander through great Gothic cathedrals almost entirely ignorant of the iconography that surrounds them, so the Japanese are increasingly becoming spectators of their own culture, rather than participants in it. The flood tide of material prosperity is sweeping the mass of the people further and further away from established religion. Still, to every action there is always some kind of reaction and, while the laws of cultural dynamics may be less predictable than those which govern the physical world, the general principle holds good. Increasing secularisation may be a major trend in contemporary Japanese society, but there are counter-currents, one of which is the growing enthusiasm for Zen among the educated young. Ultimately, of all the established Buddhist schools, Zen is probably the one most immune to harmful change. The history of Japanese painting, poetry, and theatre is inseparable from Zen, as is the progress of the Japanese aesthetic in flower arrangement, the tea ceremony, calligraphy and design. Zen is too central to everything which gives the Japanese their identity ever to fall into terminal neglect and disrepair.

Zen Buddhism may be the warp and weft of Japanese culture, but the indigenous religion of Japan, the bedrock of its religious experience, is not Buddhism at all but Shintō. Shintō is a spirit religion of a primordial type and its gods, the *kami*, are local deities, thought to be instinct with imposing natural forces or objects, such as waterfalls or trees. This essentially parochial character has enabled Shintō to be tolerant of a religion like Buddhism which is primarily concerned with a central or universal principle. Consequently the two religions have coexisted, uneasily, since the sixth century. Even today the majority of Japanese people calling themselves Buddhists (eighty-five per cent of the population) would probably also admit to being followers of Shintō.

Buddhism originally came to Japan in about AD 550 and was soon enthusiastically supported by a progressive group within society which favoured the wholesale importation of Chinese ideas and cultural forms, though the very first contact the Japanese had with Buddhism came not directly from China but from Korea. Rapidly it became the religion of the establishment and, in return for immunity from taxation and grants of land, was required to protect the State and ensure public prosperity by magic rituals. From the outset Buddhism was bound into the structure of society, made subordinate to secular authority and assumed to have the ability to control supernatural agencies.

The capital of Japan until 784 was Nara and six Buddhist sects of Chinese extraction flourished there, namely Sanron, Jōjitsu, Hossō, Kusha, Kegon and Ritsu. Of these Hossō, Kegon and Ritsu still exist, but are of relatively minor importance. While the achievements of the Nara period in architecture and sculpture were considerable – the Hōryūji temple completed in AD 607 is often held to be the finest building in Japan – it produced no religious figures of lasting importance and

Buddhism was very much a priestly affair, involving much learned study and disputation and very little contact with the people outside the monastery walls. With the removal of the capital to Kyoto however, the headquarters of the clergy was no longer the centre of government and the ground was cleared for religious innovation.

At the end of the eighth century the hills around Kyoto were wild and forested. Even today they are largely unspoiled. It was to one of them, Mount Hiei, that a monk, Saichō, retired for several years of uninterrupted study. The subject of his research was the work of a Buddhist master, Chih-i, who had lived two hundred years earlier in China's T'ien-t'ai mountains. This was both the modest beginning of the Tendai sect and the first habitation on the mountain which was soon to succeed Nara as the focal point of Japanese Buddhism. Before long, a temple replaced the hermit's cell and in 794 the Emperor Kanmu took part in a consecration ceremony, declaring that henceforward it was the 'place of practice for the protection of the state'. The absolute authority of the Nara hierarchy was at an end. Saichō was soon

Left: Pilgrims arrive by coach at Mount Kōya, the head temple of the Shingon School, founded on a mountain south of Kyoto by Kūkai in AD 816.

Right: Stone pillars and cedars in the Mount Kōya mist. Kūkai is said still to be sitting in meditation in a small building adjacent to the main temple.

commissioned to go to China to perfect his studies and on his return the Tendai sect was officially recognised and authorised to ordain novices.

Saichō's Tendai was in fact an extension, not just a translation of the T'ien-t'ai doctrine. The Chinese master had attempted to synthesise prevailing traditions, employing as his principal source of reference and inspiration the Lotus Sūtra, an Indian Mahāyāna work, subsequently of unrivalled importance in the history of Japanese Buddhism. To this theoretical basis, Saichō added both the practice of meditation and an esoteric teaching known as 'True Word' which was derived from the Indian Tantras. The Tantras cryptically describe secret rituals and techniques (held to be immensely powerful) which exerted enormous influence on both late Indian and Tibetan Buddhsim.

The introduction of the new Tendai had several far-reaching effects. Most obvious of these was the rapid development of Mount Hiei as Japan's leading academic and monastic centre, the majority of all the major Buddhist figures of the following centuries spending at least some period of their formative years there. In addition, Tendai's emphasis on meditation created interest in a more personal, less academic approach to Buddhism, preparing the way for the introduction of Zen three hundred years later by Eisai, himself a Tendai monk. (Initially however, it was the esoteric ritual aspect of Tendai which was the most widely practised part of the new doctrine.) Finally, Saichō's innovations led to the establishment at the centre of Japanese Buddhist studies of the Lotus Sūtra, a development with untold consequences for the future of Buddhism as a popular religion.

Opposite: A devotee prays at the Asakusa Kannon Temple, one of the oldest and most popular temples in Tokyo. The main hall is said to house a tiny golden statue of Kannon found by fishermen in AD 628.

The Lotus Sūtra maintains that it is not personal effort which is of primary importance in the quest for spiritual liberation. Rather, it introduces the notion of salvation achieved with the help of the bodhisattvas, those perfected beings who have chosen to remain within the cycle of rebirth for the spiritual welfare of all humanity. Nowadays Tendai is no longer a major sect (though it does exist and its headquarters are still on Mount Hiei), but the Lotus Sūtra and the doctrines of salvation which it proposes are crucial to twentieth-century Japanese Buddhism.

Accompanying Saichō on his journey to China in AD 804 was a man, Kūkai, whose influence has had no need of intermediaries. The Buddhist school which he founded, Shingon, thrives to this day, having millions of adherents. Kūkai chose to study under the Chinese master Hui-kuo, the Patriarch of the 'True Word' esoteric doctrine. Having initiated Kūkai into the secrets of this tradition, Hui-kuo died and Kūkai succeeded him as Patriarch. Returning to Japan, he began to teach and in 816 founded a temple on Mount Kōya, south of Kyoto and to this day an important centre of pilgrimage. The culmination of Kūkai's career was the construction of a Shingon temple inside the Imperial Palace, where in 834 prayers were first offered for the welfare of the Emperor. The practice of Shingon depends to a great extent on the use of ritual gestures, *mudrās*, the recitation of short formulas or prayers, *mantras*, and the pursuit of symbolic trains of thought, *kanjō*. Correct performance of rituals relying on these three techniques is intended to bring the practitioner to the realisation of the identity of his own consciousness with that of the supreme cosmic Buddha, the Ultimate Truth, known as Mahāvairocana. Kūkai regarded Shingon mysticism as the pinnacle of Buddhist religious experience, the tenth and last rung on a ladder of spiritual advancement. Early Hīnayāna Buddhism ranked only fourth.

Unless secret doctrines are strictly controlled they are open to abuse and misunderstanding and much of the lasting popularity of Shingon Buddhism among the laity seems to have been due to little more than superstition. Complex religious symbolism came to be regarded merely as a particularly potent kind of ritual magic, a tendency aided and abetted by the efforts of both the Shingon and Tendai sects to reconcile Buddhism and Shintō in a syncretism known as Ryōbu Shintō. The indigenous gods, the kami, were henceforth seen by many Japanese as avatars of Buddhas and Bodhisattvas. Indeed the sun goddess, Amaterasu Ōmikami, was held to be identical with the cosmic Buddha Mahāvairocana.

Concern for the spiritual welfare of the mass of the population continued to preoccupy the minds of leading Buddhist thinkers and towards the end of the twelfth century two academic authorities, Hōnen and Shinran, both of whom had studied with the Tendai sect on Mount Hiei, began the movement which (Shingon esotericism notwithstanding) has dominated Japanese popular Buddhism to this day: 'Pure Land', or in Japanese, *Jōdo*. The Pure Land is held to be a paradise in which one may be reborn after death. Although not itself Nirvāna, it is said to be much easier to achieve final liberation from the Pure Land than from the earthly cycle of rebirth. The superintendent deity of this paradise is Amida, the Buddha of Boundless Light, and it is through faith in him and his divine intervention that entry to the Pure Land may be gained.

Hōnen, the founder of Jōdo, was much influenced by a prevailing belief (found in the Lotus Sūtra) that the Buddha had prophesied a steady disintegration of his teaching after his death. This process of decay was thought to take place in three stages, the last and most degenerate of which, *mappō*, was calculated to have begun in AD 1052. In the age of mappō, it was supposed, the Buddha's Dharma had become so enfeebled that man was unable to attain Enlightenment by his own efforts and therefore was forced to rely on an outside agency interceding on his behalf. Although

The 184ft high pagoda of Toji Temple, Kyoto, is the tallest in Japan. Toji, a Shingon temple, was founded at the end of the eighth century, but the pagoda was rebuilt in 1641 after having been damaged by fire.

thoroughly conversant with the whole vast edifice of Mahāyāna philosophy, Hōnen decided that, given the nature of the times, what ordinary men needed in order to make spiritual progress was not religious knowledge, but intensified religious feeling. In order to generate this intensity he advocated, as a fundamental religious observance, the constant repetition of the name of Amida Buddha. The invocation (or *nembutsu*) 'Namu-Amida-Butsu', combined with fervent faith in Amida's powers of salvation would, it was hoped, be sufficient to ensure rebirth in the Pure Land.

The impetus of Hōnen's work was sustained by his disciple Shinran who further emphasised that all spiritual progress is the product of outside help, a concept known as *tariki*. Interestingly enough, Shinran's life (1173–1262) partly coincided with those of Eisai (1141–1215) and Dōgen (1200–1253), both of whom believed precisely the opposite. Both Rinzai and Sōtō Zen insist that salvation and Enlightenment can only be gained by *jiriki*, or personal discipline and effort. Making only minor clarifications to Hōnen's Jōdo, Shinran founded the sect of Jōdo-shinshū, or True Pure Land, which (the name abbreviated to Shin) is the largest Buddhist sect in Japan today. Elsewhere in Buddhism it may be thought necessary to have faith in one's teacher, or faith in the capacity of the mind for transcendent experience, but there is no suggestion that faith is required in a comprehensive sense. Even if it is true that Jōdo and Shin have departed from previous orthodoxies, their doctrines remain susceptible to a variety of interpretations. For example, although the Buddha Amida is regarded by some as an independent deity acting as a kind of saviour, he may be understood in the original Mahāyāna sense as merely an aspect of Ultimate Reality, a personifica-

tion of one attribute of Truth. Similarly, the practice of nembutsu, or invocation, can be viewed as a means by which the mind can be stilled and concentration generated.

Whether or not this is how the majority of Jōdo or Shin devotees conceive of their religion is a matter for conjecture. Some writers insist that a very small proportion of the millions of present-day Pure Land devotees would need to be disabused of the notion that Amida's paradise literally exists. On the other hand, how can one explain the disproportionate popularity of this branch of Buddhism except by reference to the obvious appeal of the doctrine of salvation without personal effort and the notion of a delightful dream world after death?

The most controversial Japanese Buddhist sect, Nichiren, has considerable affinity to those of the Pure Land, but its ideas are even less orthodox. Nichiren was born in the first quarter of the thirteenth century, the son of a poor fisherman. That more than anyone else he should have promoted the cause of Buddhist populism is therefore understandable. After ten years' training in the Tendai school on Mount Hiei, Nichiren came to the conclusion that the Lotus Sūtra was the essential part of that doctrine and moreover the purest expression of the Ultimate Truth. In particular he isolated the last fourteen chapters of the Sūtra as being of the highest possible importance. Like Hōnen however, Nichiren was greatly affected by the idea that the wisdom of the Buddhist Dharma was unknowable in the degenerate age of mappō. He feared that both the Tendai doctrine and the Lotus Sūtra were in consequence impenetrable to the ordinary man. As a remedy he declared that the very name of the Lotus Sūtra had mantric power and that constant repetition of it combined with the

One of the thirty-three manifestations of Kannon, the Japanese Bodhisattva of Compassion, in Toji Temple, Kyoto. Elsewhere, Kannon is known by the Sanskrit name, Avalokiteshvara.

Lay people entering Todaiji temple, Nara, take a drink of water as a form of ritual purification.

realisation that Buddhahood is potential in everyone, was capable of generating the highest Enlightenment. Ever since the morning of 17 May 1253, when from a hilltop Nichiren greeted the sun rising over the sea with the words 'Namu Myōhō Renge Kyō' – Homage to the Lotus Sūtra of the Wonderful Law – the invocation of this formula has been the primary religious practice of all Nichiren groups.

While Nichiren was undoubtedly concerned to promote the spiritual welfare of the individual, he chose to bring this about by political and social reform and consequently became embroiled in politics. He also began a war of attrition with all other Buddhist sects, not only demanding that they should be suppressed, but declaring them to be of diabolical origin, and the underlying causes of the imminent national collapse which he grimly foretold. Followers of the Pure Land schools responded to this assessment by setting fire to his house. Undaunted, Nichiren merely redoubled his attacks, pressing them home with even greater vitriol. Eventually he succeeded in upsetting everyone – both government and Buddhist clergy – so much that he was condemned to death. He escaped execution however, as if by a miracle, and was instead exiled for three years to an island in the Sea of Japan where he continued his religious writing. Permitted to return to the mainland, he spent the rest of his life on Mount Minobu, near Mount Fuji, consolidating the organisation of his sect.

Despite his best efforts, immediately following his death disputes broke out among his six chief disciples and one, Nikkō, set up a new group which he called Nichiren Shōshū, or The True School of Nichiren. Such a schism might well have been the end of Nichirenism as a potent force, and this strange, wrathful, arrogant man would have become just one of the more colourful footnotes to Japanese religious history. Indeed, for the next 650 years Nichirenism was a relatively minor Buddhist movement. It was not until the twentieth century that vital significance was rediscovered in its message.

By the end of the thirteenth century all the major forces which shape contemporary Japanese Buddhism schools had come into being. In the ensuing centuries no new Buddhist schools were founded and no new religious leaders emerged of the stature of Saichō, Kūkai, Hōnen, Shinran, Eisai, Dōgen and Nichiren. When in 1603, in the aftermath of civil war, the Shoguns closed Japan to foreigners, Buddhism was cut off from its constant source of inspiration in China. Things scarcely improved when the borders were opened again in 1868 at the restoration of the monarchy. In order to create a state cult, in which the Emperor was to be regarded as a direct descendant of the sun goddess Amaterasu Ōmikami, it was decreed that the indigenous religion Shintō was in need of purification and that all traces of its syncretism with Buddhism had to be ruthlessly expunged. A radical movement, *haibutsu-kishaku*, called for the complete suppression of Buddhism and although its demands went unanswered, during the enforcement of the government's policy many Buddhist temples were destroyed.

During the twentieth century there have been many attempts to modernise, liberalise and reinvigorate structures and doctrines showing signs of decadence or decay. In the universities, these efforts have met with some success. However, in a country where most of the population is still affiliated to a Buddhist temple, there has been a conspicuous lack of progress in dispelling popular apathy and introducing reform in local temples.

Counter to the general mood of pessimism prevailing since the Second World War has been an extraordinary cultural phenomenon: the rise of 'new religion'. There are in fact several new religions, all of which have roots which go back to before 1945, but it is the post-war period which has seen the remarkable expansion of one of them: Sōka Gakkai. In 1928 an educationalist called Tsunesaburō Makiguchi became converted to Nichiren Shōshū and discovered that its ideas were startlingly

Lanterns glow at dusk, Nigatsudo Temple, Nara. The parapet provides the best view of the ancient city, which was capital of Japan from 719–794.

compatible with a 'theory of values' which had been his life's work. Sōka Gakkai, founded in 1937, was the result of his fusion of the two. During the war, Makiguchi was imprisoned for refusing to co-operate with offical measures to encourage the practice of Shintō rites and in 1944, still in gaol, he died. One of his disciples, Jōsei Toda had, however, stayed with him to the end and in 1951 he was inaugurated as the second President of Sōka Gakkai. Membership of the organisation was then said to be three thousand *families*. When Toda himself died, seven years later, a quarter of a million people attended his funeral. By 1965 membership was estimated at six million families and today it is probably in excess of twenty-five million people. Sōka Gakkai now has an affiliated political party, runs a national daily newspaper, funds its own university in Tokyo, owns the largest religious building in Japan, and organises a vigorous evangelist movement in Europe and North America.

The precise reasons for this unprecedented success are difficult to identify. Nichiren Shōshū, begun by Nikkō in less than perfect circumstances in 1290, was until this century an insignificant sect. Now, absorbed by Sōka Gakkai, it is one of the largest Buddhist groups in Japan. One factor generally agreed upon is the movement's absolute belief in itself, a characteristic one can only assume to stem from the messianic self-confidence of Nichiren himself. The rites and beliefs of the religion certainly have not changed greatly: invocation of the name of the Lotus Sūtra is still of paramount importance, this being combined with worship of a mandala (sacred diagram) drawn by Nichiren himself, and said to embody the Sūtra's teaching. Each new member of Sōka Gakkai is given a reproduction of the mandala and is required to put it in a household shrine. What *has* changed is the status accorded to Nichiren himself, who is regarded by Sōka Gakkai as the Buddha of the Age of Mappō, an exalted rank hotly disputed not only by other Buddhists but by their Nichiren sects.

This has not been the only controversy to have surrounded Sōka Gakkai. An avowedly evangelistic organisation, it regards Nichiren Shōshū as the supreme religion and one of sole efficacy. As a logical consequence of this position, conversion, of the whole world if possible, is seen as a moral duty. Sōka Gakkai's chosen method of winning converts is called *shakubuku*, which is generally translated as 'break and subdue'. Though the intended meaning of this word is closer to 'persuade by passionate argument', it seems that some of the early members of the organisation were unaware of semantic niceties and took their religious zeal a little too seriously. Nowadays, in the success and prosperity of later life, Sōka Gakkai has undoubtedly mellowed. Whether this means it will continue to prosper to the same prodigious extent remains to be seen. Much of the movement's early impetus was probably derived from widespread feelings of desolation and hopelessness following Japan's defeat and invasion. It is extremely revealing therefore that in a time of crisis people did not turn to the multitude of established religious groups for comfort. Buddhism obviously had such a tenuous hold on its millions of nominal adherents that many felt impelled to forget the past and to begin again. It would be hard to maintain that the situation has altered very greatly in recent years. Only the revival of interest in Zen, partly fuelled by international fascination with this remarkable cultural tradition, has provided solid grounds for optimism about the future of Buddhism in Japan.

At thriving institutions like Eiheiji, bustling with pilgrims, it is still possible to feel, unmistakably, something ancient and unchanging. The links of tradition there seem to lead swiftly and directly back to the origin of the religion, an impression sustained by the timeless words of the monastery's present Abbot: 'Buddha's teaching must be performed in our daily lives. Sitting in meditation the Buddha is there. Everything, the whole universe, we have in our minds. If you practise you will come to believe this. Our breath is the breath of Shākyamuni Buddha.'

Opposite: The Abbot of Eiheiji, successor to the great office created by Dōgen in the thirteenth century.

Following spread: A novice monk practises *zazen*, Serene Reflection Meditation, in the *zendō* at Eiheiji.

An Open Secret

4

Tibetan Buddhism in exile

'*The most extreme happiness*
Is the self-emanation of self-power;
Happy are the myriad forms, the myriad revelations.
As a welcoming gift to my faithful pupils
I sing of yogic happiness.'

Milarepa, *The Song of the Yogi's Joy*

His Holiness the Dalai Lama invariably shakes hands with Westerners, often to the temporary confusion of those who have come prepared to bow in the Tibetan fashion, palms together, eyes lowered. The grasp is forceful, though under subsequent scrutiny his fingers turn out to be quite slender and refined. His expression, though kindly, seems strangely at odds with his voice, which is gruff and authoritative. Such subtle contradictions hint at the complexities of his position, for the Dalai Lama must equally play the parts of head of state, religious leader, and in the Tibetan Buddhist tradition, that of a manifestation of Avalokiteshvara, the universal principle of compassion.

His present home in the north Indian hill-station of Dharamsala, certainly provides very modest accommodation compared to the massive Potala palace in Tibet, which he last saw in 1959. The Audience Hall is a large, conventional living-room with a sofa, a couple of armchairs and a sizeable throne up against one wall. Two of the four attitudes which help to create superior human beings, he once remarked, are 'not wishing for fancy or colourful attire' and 'satisfaction with just enough shelter to protect oneself from the elements'. Seen from this timeless Buddhist perspective, the enforced architectural and decorative austerity of Dharamsala are really quite appropriate.

As a child in the 1940s, the Dalai Lama was so hemmed in by protocol that he was reduced to squinting at his subjects through a telescope from the roof of the Potala, five hundred feet above the streets of Lhasa. At that time Tibet was a closed country. Nowadays he is no longer inaccessible. Scholars, scientists, journalists, writers, film makers – all seem to be fitted into his schedule somehow. As a result of this openness, he has steadily acquired an international reputation, becoming not only a spokesman for his faith and his people but also a focal point for the entire Buddhist religion.

A lonely childhood was followed by exile at the age of twenty-four. In the 1960s and 70s, during the long years of the Cultural Revolution, he could do little more than watch helplessly as his country and religion were desecrated and his people slaughtered. Yet despite having seen the ancient edifice of Tibetan Buddhism shattered, his outlook is still profoundly optimistic. 'Human knowledge continually increases', he remarked equably. 'For example, some scientists are now taking a keen interest in Buddhist explanations of consciousness, so possibly such modern developments will arouse new interest in deep spiritual experience.' Even the inexorable rise

Opposite: Exiled Tibetans dance beneath the tall trees of the Himalayan foothills in Dharamsala, Northern India. Their celebrations are to mark the Tibetan New Year.

110

His Holiness the Fourteenth Dalai Lama of Tibet presides over a ritual of consecration at the new residence of the Tibetan state oracle; Dharamsala, India.

of secularism fails to dismay him: 'Material comfort may make some people forget spiritual values and religious practice, but everything depends on an individual's experience and understanding. When material development arrives, basic human problems, religious problems, these remain the same.' Asked whether he thought life in modern society could possibly be reconciled with high spiritual ambition, he positively beamed: 'Ah, that is my favourite subject! All hope for the future depends upon maintaining a reasonable balance between material and spiritual concerns. At the moment we are all preoccupied with economics, but times I am sure will change.'

Such optimism from a man who has experienced so much suffering is remarkable. There is, however, unanimous agreement among Tibetans that the present Dalai Lama is an exceptional figure. Any visitor to Dharamsala, or to any other of the Tibetan settlements for that matter, cannot fail to be impressed by the veneration and respect in which he is universally held. It seems impossible to prompt a word of criticism. At one end of the social scale, the poor, possibly illiterate, peasant regards him with a complex mixture of awe and affection. At the other, the Western-educated, senior civil servant is devoted to him both as a charismatic political leader and a man of immense spiritual authority. Whenever word gets out in Dharamsala that he is about to leave his residence to perform some religious or governmental duty, the roads are quickly lined with Tibetans waiting for the briefest glimpse as the official car swiftly passes. This enthusiasm has little to do with mere gawking. These people undoubtedly feel that just to be physically close to the Dalai Lama confers some mysterious benediction. One senior monk, commenting on the steady flow of refugees from Tibet to India, remarked 'They will continue to come. They are happy here: happy to be near His Holiness. He makes them feel secure.'

To some Westerners such overt paternalism might seem less than wholly desirable, but experiencing the groundswell of emotional warmth in Dharamsala rapidly dispels

any misgivings. Every so often the Dalai Lama holds a mass audience for his people and anyone who wishes may stand in line to receive his blessing. The crowds assemble in the tree-lined square separating his residence from the nearby Namgyal monastery and soon a queue of about two or three thousand people loops itself around the monastic buildings and small ancillary shrines. In simple red and yellow robes the Dalai Lama stands in his garden among the marigolds, patiently receiving them all for up to six or seven hours. Each person approaches, bowing reverently, and is greeted by a smile and a hand of blessing on the crown of the head. For some, often women with young children or the very old, there is a word of particular enquiry.

A Tibetan offering of flowers for the Dalai Lama, Dharamsala.

Nowhere else in the world can there be such intimate contact between the ruler and the ruled, between the supreme religious authority and the massed ranks of the faithful. Of course such an ideal arrangement is partly the product of circumstances. Were the Dalai Lama still in Tibet he could scarcely greet in person the thousands who would congregate wherever he went. Nonetheless, Dharamsala clearly demonstrates the remarkable relationship which still exists between the Dalai Lama, the Buddhist religion and the Tibetan people, a relationship which goes a long way towards justifying the frequent assertion that the Tibetans, in defiance of recent circumstances, are the most devout people anywhere in the world.

Although the Dalai Lama is indisputably the pre-eminent figure in Tibetan Buddhism, the importance of his position can be overemphasised. Following the death of each incarnation, there is necessarily an interregnum of about twenty years (until his successor attains his majority), during which the government is in the hands of a Regent and the Buddhist traditions are upheld by the Abbots of the great monasteries. It is also important to remember that the present, Fourteenth, Dalai Lama has an unusually impressive personality and sufficiently conspicuous talents to have little difficulty in asserting his authority. Not all his predecessors have been in

113

An Open Secret

Exiled members of the Gelug-pa, or 'Yellow-hat' school of Tibetan Buddhist monks at a ceremony in Dharamsala attended by the Dalai Lama, himself a Gelug-pa monk.

Previous spread: Elderly Tibetan woman prays, surrounded by juniper smoke, during ceremonies held to mark the Tibetan New Year, Dharamsala.

this fortunate position. Perhaps only the Fifth and Thirteenth have been able to exercise a similar degree of influence and power.

For hundreds of years Tibetan Buddhism progressed without any strong central control. Following its introduction from India in the seventh century AD, it was patronised by the Kings of Tibet until the reign of Lang-darma, whose persecution of Buddhism in favour of earlier, indigenous religious forms ended only with his assassination in 842. Unfortunately, as the royal line had no acknowledged heir to succeed him, a period of civil war ensued during which the kingdom broke up into a number of petty principalities. In these difficult circumstances, Buddhism virtually disappeared from central Tibet. However, as a result of a second propagation, from the tenth century onwards several distinct schools of Tibetan Buddhism came into being. One of them based itself retrospectively on the alleged teachings of a spiritual master called Padmasambhava. His adherents created the *Nyingma-pa* or Nyingma School, which claims to be the earliest of the four principal groups surviving today. The other three are the *Kargyu-pa*, founded by the teacher Marpa around 1060, the *Sakya-pa*, based on the teachings of the mystic Drogmi and named after the great monastery of Sakya during the eleventh century and the *Gelug-pa*, instituted in 1407 by arguably the most influential figure in the history of Tibetan Buddhism: Tsong-kha-pa.

The Gelug-pa began as a reform movement, reintroducing strict monastic discipline and insistence on intellectual effort as prerequisites for religious experience. Tsong-kha-pa's intentions were religious, not political, and it was no part of his plan

to come to dominate the schools already in existence. The name Gelug-pa means 'Virtuous Ones', and it was this sense of superior standards which initially kept the school aloof from the feuding periodically engaged in by the other religious orders.

During the thirteenth century, the Sakya-pa had been the first group to achieve political ascendancy when the Mongols, then the rulers of China and the strongest military force in Asia, had appointed the Abbot of Sakya as their Regent over the whole of Tibet. However, after the death of Tsong-kha-pa in 1417, the Gelug-pa continued to gain steadily in strength and the monasteries founded by its adherents rapidly became the foremost religious centres in Tibet. In 1578 the third Grand Lama of the largest of these monasteries (Drepung) accepted the honorific 'Dalai' (meaning 'Ocean of Wisdom') from a Mongol chieftain, Altan Khan. By strange coincidence, his reincarnation was subsequently discovered to be the Khan's great-grandson and in consequence the Mongols thereafter felt it appropriate to intervene in Tibetan affairs on behalf of Gelug-pa interests. The culmination of this interference came in 1642, when Gushri Khan established the fifth Dalai Lama as political ruler of the entire country by military force.

The 'Great Fifth' consolidated Geluga-pa power, building the vast Potala Palace in Lhasa as a symbol of its magnificence, and became the architect of the theocracy which governed Tibet until the Chinese invasion in 1950. Not until early this century, two hundred years after his death, was there however a successor to his office whose influence was in any way comparable.

Tibetan refugees, recently arrived in India, offer ceremonial white scarves, or *khatas*, as a gesture of respect and devotion to their leader, the Dalai Lama.

Today in Dharamsala, confronted by the adulation accorded to the ruling Dalai Lama, it is sometimes hard not to envisage chaos and disintegration following his eventual death. This is a prospect which he himself has emphatically rejected, expressing complete faith in the vitality of religious tradition independent of any one personality. His optimism seems well-founded. Despite the disasters which have befallen Tibetan Buddhism over the past thirty years, there are still many lamas of great stature, well able to carry on as their predecessors did for centuries.

When Westerners first came into contact with Tibetan Buddhism they termed it 'Lamaism'. To some of these travellers and scholars it seemed that they had encountered a religion so unlike the Buddhism familiar from South-east Asia, that it must be something altogether different. Although they were puzzled by Tibetan Buddhism's elaborate rituals and astonished by the vast pantheon of gods, goddesses, saints and demons which it embraced, what seemed to them most distinctive was the religion's preoccupation with the figure of the reincarnate lama. The word 'lama' simply means a senior religious figure. However, Tibetan Buddhism to a large extent revolves around leading spiritual practitioners who are considered to be, in an extremely direct way, reincarnations of their predecessors. For example, a child may be recognised as a reincarnation partly because he is able to identify correctly some of the material possessions that he owned in a previous existence. This kind of identification is without parallel in other forms of Buddhism where rebirth according to the laws of karma is held to be a fact, but not one about which it is easy to be specific. No other Buddhist school goes to the lengths employed by the Tibetans to convert speculation about reincarnation into a precise science.

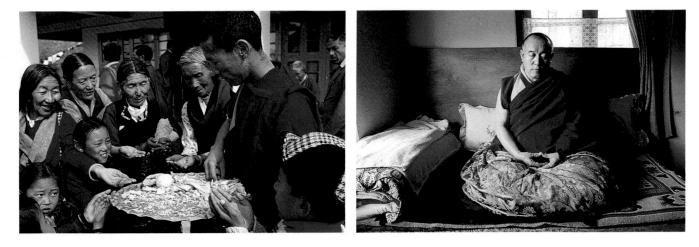

The accuracy with which new incarnations can be identified often depends partly on the ability of great religious practitioners to determine themselves both the moment and the circumstances of their death. Tibetan Buddhists believe that a highly religious man can achieve such complete control over his mind through meditation that he can enter death with, so as to speak, his eyes fully open. Death can therefore be experienced as merely a point on a continuum which marks the transition from one form of consciousness to another. The precise nature of the intermediate consciousness preceding rebirth is extensively described in the famous *Tibetan Book of the Dead*, or *Bardo Thödrol*, a work which originated in the Nyingma School. While many of its assertions may seem implausible to a modern Western mind, it is worth remembering that the psychologist Jung found them very revealing indeed. He kept the Bardo Thödrol by his bedside and claimed to have been greatly influenced by it.

Tibetan Buddhism's detractors have invariably claimed that this attitude to

reincarnation has little to do with Buddhism and that it is one of the more striking illustrations of how fatally the Tibetan tradition is comprised by magical beliefs which it inherited from Tibet's indigenous folk-religion. Certainly from the outset Tibetan Buddhism dealt with the magical. Much of the reputation of Padmasambhava, one of the first great figures in the religion's history, is based on his alleged talents as a sorcerer, and legend has it that only by his triumphant conquest and conversion of native spirits was Buddhism able to spread to Tibet. He, in other words, cleared a wilderness of demons so that the seed of the Dharma could flourish. Whether or not this story is just a metaphor which developed to describe and account for the replacement of primitive beliefs by the more sophisticated Indian religion is a matter for some dispute. Many Tibetans do believe in a spirit world and all maintain that it is possible through training and concentration to acquire abilities which most Westerners would regard as supernatural.

Left: Young Tibetans at a dance performance at Khampagar Monastery near Dharamsala.

Right: A yogi, who generally lives as a solitary hermit, joins monks in reading the scriptures at the Tibetan New Year celebrations, Khampagar Monastery.

In 1931 the French Tibetologist, Alexandra David-Neel, published her famous book, *With Mystics and Magicians in Tibet*, in which she expressed her conviction that, from her own experience, many superficially improbable Tibetan claims were indeed true. Solitary meditators living high in the Himalayas do seem, for example, to be able to raise their body temperature by a practice known as *tum-mo*, which enables them to survive the winter in freezing caves, wearing few clothes and with almost nothing to eat. Far more importantly however, she described her own experience of Tibetan techniques known collectively as 'visualisation'. Tibetans believe that through meditation, through the power of mental concentration, it is possible to have access to an alternative spiritual reality, equally 'real' to the one which we habitually assume we inhabit, but far more suited to the attainment of spiritual liberation. Their claims are based on the ideas of the classical Indian Mahāyāna schools of philosophy, the Mādhyamika and the Yogācāra, which assert that everyday physical reality is illusory, empty, and that the world we commonly perceive is purely the product of Mind. This being the case, the Tibetans seek to employ the creative power of imagination to construct an alternative realm which is similarly devoid of inherent existence, but which nonetheless corresponds far more exactly to the deepest levels of the human psyche. This realm is the one portrayed in Tibetan frescoes and religious art and is the one peopled by the extraordinary pantheon of Tibetan deities which so astonished early Western travellers. These gods and goddesses are not real, but through meditation and imagination they appear to be as real as a table or a chair commonly do – tables and chairs being themselves, in an ultimate sense, equally the products of Mind. Once brought into existence by the imagination, the help of these

Opposite: The five-year-old re-incarnate lama of Khampagar Monastery.   123

deities may be invoked in the pursuit of spiritual refinement, a technique of meditation known as 'Deity Yoga', and one regarded by Tibetan Buddhists as being of unrivalled effectiveness in the arduous pursuit of Enlightenment.

Tibetans claim that their religion is the most refined and complex Buddhist school of all. Their self-confidence stems from the fact that practically the whole extent of Indian Buddhist philosophy and literature, the fruit of centuries of spiritual experience, is preserved in the Tibetan Buddhist texts.

By the end of the twelfth century, Buddhism had largely disappeared from India. For hundreds of years, however, the Tibetans had been collecting and translating Indian texts. These were now edited into two great collections: the *Kanjur*, 108 volumes regarded as the word of the Buddha, and the *Tanjur*, 225 volumes of treatises and commentaries by Indian masters. Of course much Hīnayāna and Mahāyāna Buddhism was also preserved in Chinese translation, but the Tibetan canon is held to be more comprehensive, certainly as far as later Indian Mahāyāna is concerned. The full extent of what Tibetan libraries contained is still unclear to Western scholars. Ironically the Chinese invasion, during which tens of thousands of manuscripts were incinerated, may well have had the unintended effect of making much more available to the West. The Tibetans brought what they could with them and these texts are now far more freely accessible than perhaps would otherwise have been the case.

The enormous differences between early Buddhism and the Tibetan schools are obvious. What is less self-evident is the gulf that once separated the Hīnayāna schools from Indian Mahāyāna Buddhism, towards the end of the latter's development. Rather than simply being an exotic fruit grown in the spiritually fertile soil of Tibet, Tibetan Buddhism is an accurate reflection of the religion practised south of the Himalayas in the eleventh to twelfth centuries AD. This is why the Tibetans regard themselves as the perpetuators of the mainstream of Buddhism. Their translators took

the Indian texts of an Indian religion and lifted them to safety just before they were obliterated from their native land. Once over the mountains in their new home, the texts were preserved and regarded as sacred.

From a Tibetan perspective, Buddhism progressed over centuries, becoming an ever more subtle and powerful instrument for spiritual achievement. The Hīnayāna was excellent, so far as it went, but inevitably it was replaced by the far more sophisticated Mahāyāna. Ultimately however, the Mahāyāna was itself superseded by practices known variously as Mantrāyana, Vajrayāna, Tantrayāna or simply Tantric Buddhism. Unfortunately what Tibetans regard as a logical refinement of the doctrine has often been viewed elsewhere as a decline into decadence. Tantric Buddhism, critics maintain, is just Mahāyāna philosophy corrupted by magical practices derived from Hinduism.

Tantra evidently became part of Indian Buddhism shortly before the period when the Tibetans were energetically engaged in translation. The precise origin of the Buddhist Tantric texts (or the Hindu ones) is obscure. The earliest known examples seem to come from the sixth century AD. However, by the time of Buddhism's disappearance from India it had long ceased to be Hīnayāna and Mahāyāna presenting themselves as alternatives. The choice lay between Mahāyāna and Tantrayāna. The latter offers a programme of action, and differs fundamentally from everything that had preceded it in Indian Buddhism by its startling assertion that certain techniques enable Enlightenment to be achieved in the course of a single lifetime. The incomprehensible eons, the countless lives, that Buddhism had traditionally insisted were required to achieve Nirvāna, were now truncated, in the case of a few skilled adepts, to a few brief years. Tantra, its proponents maintain, is the highest and most powerful form of Buddhist practice. Precisely because of this immense power, it is not without dangers, and therefore its methods must be kept secret and only gradually imparted by a spiritual master, a *guru*.

A newly constructed Tibetan gompa, or temple, near Dharamsala. Over the years the refugees have come to build in a more permanent manner.

125

Left: The ancient stupa of Svayambhūnāth, Kathmandu, Nepal. The site has been of religious importance for more than 2,500 years and may have been visited by Emperor Aśoka in the third century.

Right: At Svayambhūnāth, prayer wheels are inscribed with the mantra *Om Mani Padme Hum*, 'Hail to thee, Jewel at the Heart of the Lotus'.

What then is Tantra? Being based on secret practices, revealed only to initiates, much of Tantric Buddhism remains enigmatic. For example, the Tantric texts themselves employ an elaborate symbolic language which is largely unintelligible without prior explanation or the appropriate commentaries. Nonetheless, certain general observations can be made. Tibetan Tantric Buddhism deals with psycho-physical experience. It seeks to effect spiritual transformation by using all available human resources, both mental and physical. To achieve a progressive realisation of higher mental states, the most fundamental sources of energy, for example sexual energy, may be tapped, controlled and employed through meditation. The techniques of Tantric meditation involve the progressive visualisation of deities which correspond to elements of human psychology. These deities may be thought of as the *dramatis personae* in a drama which is human consciousness. They may be benign or they may be wrathful, but through techniques of concentration their presence will be experienced with tremendous intensity. Tantra is therefore a process in which the roles habitually assigned to mind and body become confused, merged. A system constructed on the basis of Mahāyāna philosophical conclusions about the nature of mind, consciousness and Ultimate Reality, Tibetan Tantra takes the practitioner down a carefully defined road toward a final transforming realisation of the truth of these conclusions.

Opposite: A discussion of Buddhist scriptures at the Golden Temple in Patan, near Kathmandu. The predominantly Hindu Kathmandu valley has developed a distinctive religious syncretism.

Previous spread: Within sight of the summit of Mount Everest, the Nyingma-pa Monastery of Thyangboche, Nepal, is an important religious centre for the Buddhist Sherpa people.

In the past, Tibetan Tantric Buddhism was a mysterious religion from a forbidden country and the secrecy which surrounded it sometimes led to the regrettable impression in the outside world that there must be something to hide. Past generations, with markedly different preconceptions from the present, encountered Tantric sexual symbolism and immediately had all their worst suspicions confirmed. Recently this has all begun to change. Allied to Tibetan efforts to reconstruct their heritage in exile have been joint ventures with foreign scholars. Tantric texts have been published, translations made and explanations of the secret symbolism have for the first time been forthcoming. An even more spectacular illustration of this new openness has been the large-scale public initiations carried out by the Dalai Lama. The first of these in Europe took place in July 1985 at Rikon in Switzerland, a small town where several hundred Tibetan refugees were resettled in the early 1960s. Six thousand people attended the twelve-day ceremony, during which the Dalai Lama conducted the preliminary rituals for one of the most important of all the Tantras, the *Kālachakra*, said to contain the antidotes to all hindrances to Enlightenment. Although the advanced meditations of the *Kālachakra* can only be accomplished by skilled spiritual practitioners, an initiation for such a large body of people is held to be

of great significance because it establishes a 'karmic link' between the audience and the Tantra. In other words, merely attending an initiation is said to plant seeds which will come to fruition in future lives. Although the Dalai Lama conducted the ceremonies in Tibetan, there were simultaneous translations into English, French, German, Italian and Spanish.

Such events, and the underlying attitudes of which they are the result, are of the greatest possible significance for the future of Tibetan Buddhism. The fundamentally distinctive aspects of the religion are now being freely exposed to public scrutiny after having been hidden for centuries. Far from seeing this change as a concession extracted by a curious world, the Dalai Lama regards it with complete equanimity as an almost inevitable development: 'Once Mahāyāna Buddhism has been accepted as very extensive, very deep and very precise, then there is a natural attraction to the Tantric teaching for its own quality and sophistication. As a result it becomes ever more popular and then, finally, open for everyone: an open secret.'

Left: Nepali farmers give their water-buffalo a bath in the Bagmati river, near Kathmandu.

Right: Prayer flags flutter above the rooftops of Namche Bazaar in the Khumbu region of the Nepal Himalaya. Prayers written on the flags are disseminated by the wind.

Despite the unmistakable impetus of this remark – a desire to extend the benefits of Tibetan Buddhism to as great a number of people as possible – the bedrock of the tradition must remain a vigorous and disciplined monastic culture. In Tibet, the most important monasteries near the Dalai Lama's palace in Lhasa were those of Sera, Drepung and Ganden. These great institutions were refounded by the Tibetans in exile on land given to them by the Indian government, but they are all in the southern Indian state of Karnataka, over a thousand miles from their spiritual leader and his administration in the foothills of the Himalayas. Regrettably, this is far from being the most severe of the Tibetans' problems, chief among which is lack of money. There are now thousands of Tibetans monks at forty centres in eleven Indian states. These monasteries can, however, no longer rely on the social system that prevailed in Tibet, which provided all the necessities of their daily life. Today monasteries have to be self-sufficient. Many of the problems which confronted the religious authorities in the 1960s – such as widespread chronic ill-health – have been dealt with, but there is as yet no clear answer to the danger of declining standards due to the monks having to spend much of their time either at work in the fields or engaged in other financially profitable activities.

One of the chief functions of the principal Tibetan monasteries has always been religious instruction. For the student monk in a Gelug-pa monastery, an average day begins with the rising bell at 5.00 am and two hours of meditation. After breakfast there are prayers, which continue until 9.00. For the remainder of the morning, the monks attend classes on either religious ritual or important Buddhist texts. All such

Opposite: A Nepali woman lights tiny butter lamps as an offering at a small shrine beside the stupa at Svayambhūnāth.

Previous spread: Silhouetted in gentle evening light Svayambhūnāth looks out across the Kathmandu valley. In the thirteenth century Svayambhūnāth was an important centre of Buddhist learning with close links to Lhasa, in Tibet.

A mother leads her child through the narrow streets of Leh, the capital of Ladakh.

Opposite: An outdoor classroom for novices at Shey Monastery, Ladakh, north-west India. Although politically part of India, the cultural and religious life of Ladakh is almost identical to that of neighbouring Tibet.

Women wearing
traditional costume in
the courtyard of Hemis
Monastery.

lessons have to be memorised as without such detailed learning it is considered inappropriate to engage in abstract philosophical discussion. Lunch is followed by an hour-long debate, during which groups of monks test each other's knowledge of the Buddhist scriptures and philosophy. In the afternoon there are further classes and, from 5.00 until 6.30, another debating session. Dinner is followed by an hour's revision of the texts memorised that morning, after which the monks may either retire to bed or pursue their own meditation in private.

In Tibet there were no centres of learning other than the monasteries, but in India today the majority of Tibetan children receive a secular education, many subjects presently being taught in English. It is freely admitted by the Dharamsala administration that the religious authorities will never again play a dominant role in education, no matter how favourable future political conditions turn out to be, and it is also taken for granted that in any future Tibetan state there would have to be many fewer monks than there were before the Chinese invasion. Once as many as thirty percent of male Tibetans were in religious orders, but a modern society cannot function economically under such circumstances and anyway, the Dalai Lama has made it quite plain that from now on he is interested solely in the quality of the religious life of monasteries, not in the number of their inhabitants.

The decision to become a monk was traditionally made between the ages of seven and twelve, when a novice entered his local monastery. After having learned to read and write, and having memorised the basic texts, a young monk would decide whether or not to pursue his studies by going to one of the large teaching monasteries affiliated to his sect. In the case of the Gelug-pa, these were principally Drepung, Sera, and Ganden – all near Lhasa. An aspiring student might therefore have had to travel for weeks under difficult conditions just to enrol. He would then have begun a monastic curriculum divided into fifteen classes, each lasting one year. This led up to

an examination for the title of *geshe* roughly equivalent to a Doctor of Divinity degree. The first class was a year's general introduction known as *Collected Topics*. This was followed by five years devoted to the *Prajñā-pāramitā*, the classical Indian 'Perfection of Wisdom' literature, two years of *Mādhyamika*, the crucially important second-century school of Mahāyāna Buddhist philosophy, two years of the *Abhidharma*, general early Buddhist philosophy and psychology, and a year of the *Vinaya*, or monastic discipline. This preliminary part of the course completed, the monk would then begin four years' specific preparation for the arduous geshe degree by wide reading and assiduous practice of his debating skills. Only those most successful in the examination would then be eligible for admission to a Tantric College where they would spend a further five years studying the Tantric texts and learning new techniques and rituals.

Of course relatively few monks rose to these scholastic heights and some of the smaller monasteries were doubtless very far from being centres of academic excellence. The present intention of the Tibetan religious authorities is, so far as possible, to make *all* monasteries pursue a demanding programme of study. Their task is, therefore, not only to maintain standards at the highest level in the face of adverse economic circumstances, but also to broaden the base of achievement so as to include everyone in religious orders.

All such plans for the future must unfortunately take account of the depressing overall position in which the Tibetans still find themselves. Before 1959 there were over six thousand monasteries in Tibet. Now in India there are barely as many Tibetan monks. Tibetan Buddhism is still a religion in crisis, fighting for its survival, even if it shows no sign whatever of giving up the struggle.

Although the Tibetan monasteries in exile are widely scattered, there are nonetheless three principal clumps of them – in South India near Mysore, around

Recently completed Tantric statue at Thikse monastery, Ladakh.

Following spread: Built in the fifteenth century, Thikse monastery dominates the skyline beyond a small group of stupas, or *chörtens*. These generally contain a relic of a lama (or religious teacher).

137

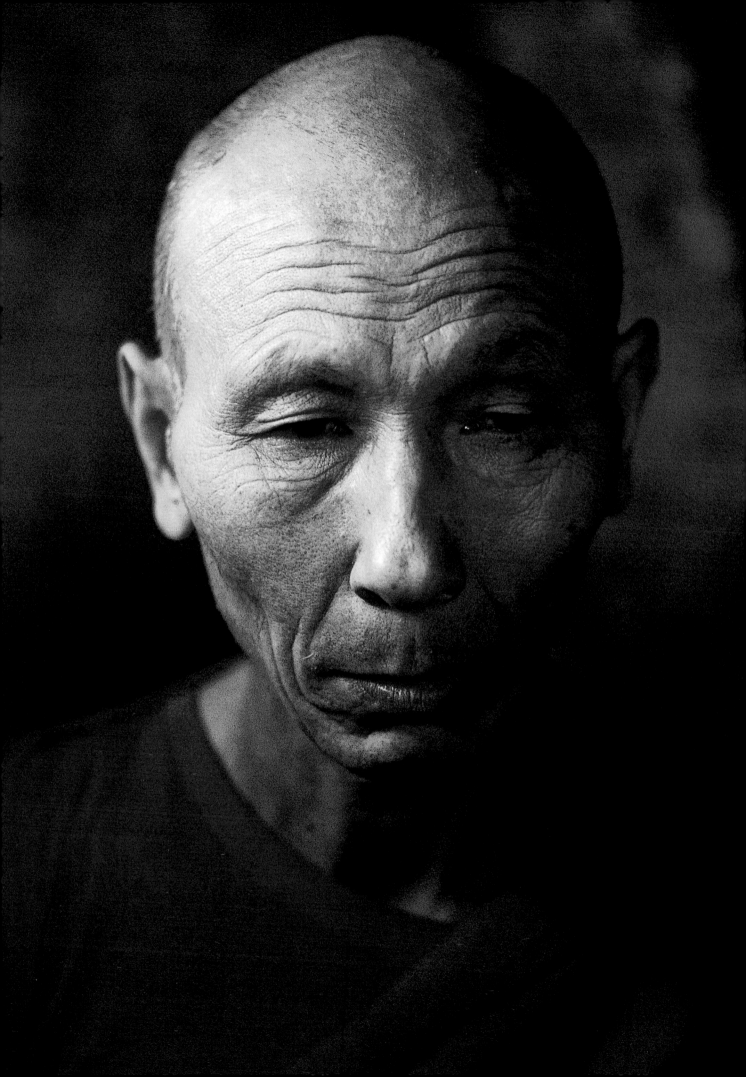

Darjeeling in West Bengal and in the foothills of the Himalayas directly north of Delhi. Dharamsala, for example, is by no means the only old hill-station to see a new influx of foreign residents. There are now Tibetan monasteries in Dalhousie, Manali, Simla, Rajpur and Mussorie, small towns famous half a century ago as the summer quarters of the British Raj. In addition there are the Tibetan Buddhist communities in the north Indian state of Ladakh, among the Sherpa people of Nepal and in the isolated Himalayan kingdom of Bhutan. These areas were subject to Tibetan influence in past centuries, and despite subsequent autonomy chose to retain their Tibetan Buddhist culture.

Precisely what fate has in store for Tibetan Buddhism, both for its institutions and for its role as a popular religion is, to say the least, problematic. In an atmosphere of continuing uncertainty it is therefore reassuring to discover that perhaps the most remarkable aspect of the Tibetan Buddhist tradition continues to prosper in exile.

For centuries many of the greatest Tibetan religious practitioners have sought spiritual fulfilment not within the confines of a monastery, but in a cave or hut high in the Himalayas, isolated from their fellow men. Most famous of these recluses was Tibet's great eleventh-century yogic poet, the visionary genius Milarepa. The extraordinary way of life celebrated in his *Hundred Thousand Songs* has subsequently been practised by countless others, driven by the urgency of their spiritual quest. Such people seem to have a special significance for the Dalai Lama, as he sits in Dharamsala surrounded by tedious protocol and the requirements of public duty: 'In future I think some monks should involve themselves in social work as has been the case in Christian orders, but some must also remain in the high mountains, as is the Tibetan tradition. Around Dharamsala, there are meditators who have spent fifteen, twenty, even thirty years alone and as a result they have had extraordinary experiences. Sometimes they come here to tell me about them.'

In a jeep it takes less than half an hour from the Dalai Lama's Residence up to the cave of Phenpo Drupthop – 'the Accomplished One from Phenpo'. In fact it not so much a cave as an overhang of rock extended with a tarpaulin and two or three sheets of corrugated iron. Inside there is no furniture, only a pallet, a pan, a kettle, a bag of tea, two eggs, a razor and a copy of Tsong-kha-pa's *Lam Rim*. Here the hermit lives, meditating for sixteen hours a day, sleeping for six or seven hours each night, leaving only one hour in twenty-four for cooking, washing and reading. So great is the mental control he has gained over his body that he hardly needs to eat, or to exercise. In winter, protected by his tum-mo practice, he scarcely feels the cold.

Fifty-six years old, he has now lived alone for more than fifteen years. After a period of study in Dharamsala he decided to become a hermit and began receiving instruction on thought transformation, purification practices and Tantric techniques. Progressively he learned how to destroy all obstacles to the Mind of Enlightenment. The first ten years of his seclusion were spent practising what is known as the 'generation stage'. Now he is in the middle of the 'completion stage' at the end of which he hopes to achieve the 'excellent accomplishment': Enlightenment.

In his lonely cave Phenpo Drupthop perpetuates the most ancient and fundamental of all Buddhist traditions, that of the man alone, wrestling with his mind to achieve a final and ultimately meaningful illumination. He is a reminder of the Buddha himself beneath the Bo-tree at Bodh Gaya. His words, spoken with serene conviction, provide heartening evidence that one of the most extraordinary aspects of the Tibetan Buddhist tradition is in little immediate danger of extinction:

'From my own experince I have found the teachings of the Buddha to be both true and reliable. They are undoubtedly an excellent way to gain peace of mind.'

Opposite: The hermit, Phenpo Drupthop, has spent more than fifteen solitary years in a cave near Dharamsala learning to destroy all obstacles to the Mind of Enlightenment.

Following spread: Phenpo Drupthop, 'the Accomplished One from Phenpo' sitting in meditation in his cave. Every day he meditates for sixteen hours.

5

Decline and Destruction

The fate of Buddhism in China and Tibet

'The officers of the state, ecclesiastical and secular, will find their lands seized and their other property confiscated, and they themselves made to serve their enemies, or wander about the country as beggars do. All beings will be sunk in great hardship and in overpowering fear; the nights and the days will drag on slowly in suffering.'   Thubten Gyatso, 13th Dalai Lama of Tibet

Early April in Beijing, and the cruel northern winter seems finally to have ended. The wind from the Mongolian steppes still blows incessantly, swirling up the dust and insinuating it into the eyes of a million cyclists, but somehow it lacks its former ferocity, the knife-like chill against which no amount of padding was proof. Fayuan Si appears deserted. The doors are padlocked, the paint is peeling, and the flower beds are the same consistency as the pavement after six months of frost. There is no-one about. Peering in through grimy windows it is possible to make out just a few piles of yellowing books perched on the edge of the darkness which fills most of the room.

First built in AD 696 during the Tang Dynasty, Fayuan Si is one of the most important Buddhist centres in the People's Republic of China, housing not only the Beijing Buddhist Academy, but also the publishing department of the Chinese Buddhist Association. Financed by the State, it is one of a hundred or so Buddhist temples that remain active in China today; in the 1920s there were approximately 130,000. Among China's billion or so inhabitants there are now about 2,500 monks; before the Second World War there were around half a million. What these seemingly self-explanatory figures fail to make clear, however, is the relative improvement of the past decade. Within two or three years of the foundation of the People's Republic in 1949, all land owned by Buddhist orders had been confiscated, destroying the Sangha's income and making it virtually impossible for monks to devote their time to study or meditation. The Sangha's very existence was in future to be completely dependent on the largesse of the State. Former monastic landowners were brought before public meetings and 'criticised', an often violent ritual of humiliation. Some were executed. Buddhist buildings were next to go, generally being requisitioned for government offices. Broad hints were dropped that monks should voluntarily disrobe and begin to contribute to Socialist construction. Within ten years, probably ninety percent of the Sangha had accepted the *fait accompli* and returned to lay life. In 1957 it was decreed that there would be no further ordinations and an 1,800-year-old tradition abruptly ended. Not that things stopped there. At the outbreak of the Cultural Revolution in 1966, the few remaining temples were closed, all monks forcibly secularised, and religious observances prohibited.

By comparison, the present state of affairs is positively ideal. As a result of the recent political thaw, Fayuan Si is now a kind of university where all the major Buddhist

Opposite: A monk practises calligraphy at Fayuan Si, Beijing, China.

schools are taught. There are over a hundred monks, and about eighty students, five of whom, in 1986, were permitted to visit Sri Lanka. In addition it has been mooted, albeit tentatively, that Oriental philosophy (and therefore the Buddhist contribution to it) should be more widely taught in China's academic curriculum as a supplement to the Marxist orthodoxy.

Despite the external appearance of neglect, presumably due to lack of money, the interior of both the Dharma Hall and the Meditation Hall at Fayuan Si bear witness to an active religious community. They are both neat and well-swept and there is the kind of sheen upon the wooden floor imparted by the daily friction of stockinged feet. The monks study for three hours in the morning and four hours in the afternoon. There is a service at 5.30 am and another at 7.00 pm. In the evening there is also an hour's meditation. The institution seems to have some kind of future ahead of it, even though its activities will doubtless be circumscribed. Buddhism as a scholastic discipline is evidently tolerated nowadays. What is certainly not envisaged is a Sangha numbering more than a few thousand, or the resumption of a relationship between the clergy and the population at large.

Two and a half thousand miles south-west of Beijing, in the Chinese Autonomous Region of Tibet, the past thirty years have witnessed a similar, though in many ways even more cataclysmic, devastation. On New Year's Day 1950, only three months after the creation of the People's Republic, Radio Peking announced that the coming year was to see the 'liberation' of Tibet by the Chinese armed forces. Within eighteen months Lhasa was under their control. At first the Dalai Lama and the Tibetan civil administration attempted to co-operate, hoping that if the Chinese enjoyed military security on their western borders, they might be prepared to let the Tibetans go about their own business in peace. It rapidly became apparent that this was not to be the case and relations steadily deteriorated until finally, in 1959, the Tibetans staged an

abortive armed revolt. To retain any freedom of action the Dalai Lama was obliged to flee to India.

In the years that followed, the pattern established in China was repeated in Tibet and the destruction of the Buddhist Sangha, the demolition of its buildings and the confiscation of its property was soon under way. Monasteries were stormed using artillery and then blown up. Of the more than six thousand which existed before the invasion, fewer than one hundred remain. Hundreds of monks died in their defence. Thousands more were sent away to labour camps. Many were simply shot.

The most terrible scenes of destruction are at Ganden, 14,000 feet up in the mountains, forty miles to the east of Lhasa. The oldest of the three principal Gelug-pa monasteries (the other two being Drepung and Sera), Ganden was established in 1409 by Tsong-kha-pa, the great Tibetan religious reformer. Because of its historical importance, it seems to have provoked an attack of particular fury. Once the home of about five thousand monks, it is now a miniature Dresden, a roofless labyrinth of shattered masonry. Officially no monks are permitted to live there, but in defiance of authority about 150 have returned to endure a troglodyte existence, sheltered from the bitter cold at high altitude by walls crudely reconstructed from the rubble and a few sheets of patched and faded tarpaulin. Dozens of pilgrims visit them every day, many of whom climb the two thousand feet to the monastery on their hands and knees, prostrating in the dust both to improve their karma by acquiring merit and to express their particular veneration for one of the most sacred places of their religion.

Materialist ideology in general and the Cultural Revolution in particular have had traumatic consequences for Buddhism in both China and Tibet. The political theory has been the same in both cases and the methods employed have been extremely similar. Yet the consequences have been entirely different. In China the population has acquiesced in the dismemberment of the religion, and there now seems little

At Fayuan Si in Beijing young monks practise meditation.

Following spread:
Wrapped up against the bitter cold, a monk crosses the garden of Fayuan Si.

Ganden monastery, Tibet. Mounted on a silver stupa is one of the teeth of Tsong-kha-pa, the great religious reformer and founder of the Gelug School. Small pieces of paste made from barley flour are given the impression of the tooth, dried in the sun, and then sold to pilgrims.

Opposite: A recently painted fresco of Tsong-kha-pa, at Drepung Monastery, Lhasa.

Previous spread: Ruins of a Buddhist monastery in southern Tibet. The vast majority of Tibet's monasteries have been destroyed since 1959.

Decline and Destruction

Yonghe Gong Temple, Beijing, China. An inscription of the temple's name in (right to left) Manchu, Chinese, Tibetan and Mongol characters. The Manchu emperors of China practised the Tibetan form of Buddhism.

prospect of Buddhism re-emerging as a force of any real consequence in society. In Tibet, however, the piety of the people seems to have been strengthened by adversity. Of course this is partly because, in Tibet, church and state have been connected for hundreds of years and the Buddhist Sangha is inextricably bound up with the Tibetan desire for self-determination. Nonetheless it would be untrue to say that continued Tibetan devotion to the Buddhist religion is mostly the result of frustrated nationalism. On the contrary, the Tibetans seem to be a uniquely devout people, in whom the religious instinct is, if anything, even stronger than the national one.

The reasons for the same policy having opposite effects in two parts of what is now the People's Republic are found in the history of Buddhism north of the Himalayas. Not only are the Chinese and the Tibetans racially and linguistically separate peoples, their respective cultures have, for the most part, developed independently. Buddhism came to China and Tibet at different times and partly by different routes and, whereas Tibetans have always practised late-Indian Buddhism, in China all the major movements of the Mahāyāna have flourished.

Legend tells us that Buddhism was brought to China from India by envoys of Emperor Ming who ruled from AD 58 to 75. After several years abroad, they returned with scriptures, an Indian Buddhist master and a white horse. Delighted by the success of their mission, the Emperor founded for them the Monastery of the White Horse near the city of Luoyang, then capital of China. Although the monastery still exists, regrettably its buildings are from a later age and it is now agreed that the whole

story is a fable concocted to account neatly for an untidy process of cultural transfer which took place over an extended period of time. It is generally accepted that Buddhism did not come directly from India at all, but rather travelled along the Silk Road from Central Asia. Certainly towards the end of the second century, the translation of Buddhist scriptures was under way in Luoyang, but for the next 150 years such work was carried out on a limited scale and Buddhism made little impression on the mainstream of Chinese civilisation.

Unlike some countries to which Buddhism was to spread, China already had a mature culture and indigenous religion. In these circumstances it was unlikely that Buddhism would spread rapidly of its own accord. It is one of the grand coincidences of world history that the sixth century BC saw the lives of not only the Buddha, but also of Lao Tsu and Confucius and it was with the influence of these two great Chinese sages that Buddhism was destined to compete. Taoism, the religion based on Lao Tsu's work, the *Tao Te Ching*, had developed both as a popular religion of magic and ritual and as a refined spiritual philosophy, in many ways comparable with the speculations of Mahāyāna Buddhism. It was Confucianism, however, which had had the greater effect on the Chinese collective psyche, and it was an effect which Buddhism was never able to obviate. China never became a Buddhist country, and Buddhism was only ever one among three rival systems which were obliged, uneasily, to coexist.

Though more a political and social philosophy than a religion, Confucianism is based on the idea that the ruler is sanctified by the 'Mandate of Heaven', and is required to maintain on earth the divinely inspired order of the universe. Its most

The Yonghe Gong is one of Beijing's most active Buddhist temples. Originally built as a palace, it was rededicated as a Buddhist temple in 1723.

Following spread: An elderly monk at a Jiuhua Shan monastery stands next to the Chinese character for Buddha. Jiuhua Shan is one of China's four sacred mountains. The other three are Emei, Wutai and Putuo.

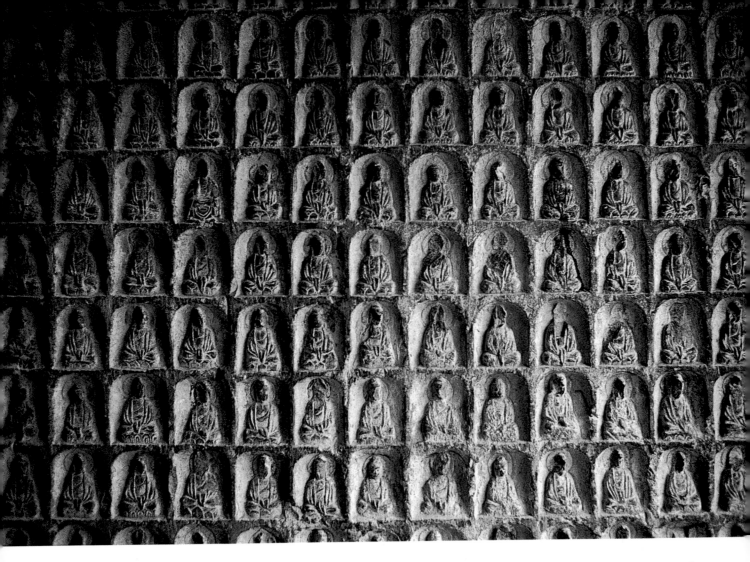

The Cave of the Ten
Thousand Buddhas at
the Longmen Caves,
Luoyang.

Previous spread: Evening
ceremony at one of the
sixty temples on Jiuhua
Shan, the 'Nine Flower
Mountain'. Power cuts
are frequent, and
hurricane-lamps provide
the most reliable form of
illumination.

fundamental values are, therefore, those of stability and harmony which are to be engendered by each individual's sense of social duty and conformity to prescribed rules of behaviour. It is a philosophy which elevates the role of the state and places restrictions on the freedom of the individual. Because of this preference it is inimical to the spirit of Buddhism, which exalts individual spiritual experience, seeing the forms and observances of society as serious obstacles to self-realisation. Furthermore, a less Confucian institution than the Buddhist Sangha would be hard to envisage: an influential organisation entirely separate from the State, owing the latter no allegiance, promoting a contradictory set of values, not liable to taxation, unproductive of material goods, and composed of pacifist ascetics ineligible for civil or military service.

Buddhism's opportunity to prosper in spite of the prevailing ethos took some while to arrive. As long as the Chinese State was secure, its citizens dutiful and the heavens fulfilling their side of the Confucian bargain by ensuring peace and plenty, the foreign interloper was unlikely to be paid very much attention. It was not until the advent of a period of disunity and strife, when conventional wisdom might be seen to have failed, that new ideas would be countenanced. In Chinese history the period from AD 311 to 589 was one in which large tracts of territory came to be ruled by invaders from elsewhere in Asia, the central authority of the Empire having disintegrated. By the time it was reconstituted under the Sui Dynasty, and the borders once more secured, Buddhism had become a force to be reckoned with.

It was around the middle of the fourth century that Buddhism was first adopted as the religion of the aristocracy and intelligentsia. In about AD 380 the ruler of the Jin territory in southern China vowed to adhere to the Buddhist lay precepts, and in consequence patronage of the Sangha, chiefly in grants of land, quickly gathered momentum. (At this time Buddhism also expanded into Korea, from where it spread

to Japan two hundred years later.) A further event of tremendous significance was the arrival, in 402, of the Indian scholar Kumārajīva at Chang'an, now Xi'an. During the next ten years, hundreds of scholars were sponsored by the state to translate, under his supervision, some three hundred Buddhist works including the Diamond Sūtra and the Lotus Sūtra. It was also Kumārajīva who introduced the Chinese to Mādhyamika, the central philosophy of Mahāyāna Buddhism, the fundamental doctrine of which, Shūnyatā ('Emptiness') came to provide the theoretical basis for Chan Buddhism, known in Japan as Zen.

In response to these developments, all over China there was a flurry of construction: monasteries, pagodas, and most magnificent of all, huge cave temples with towering statuary. At one of the largest of these complexes, Longmen, near the city of Luoyang, approximately one hundred thousand images were carved in one thousand three hundred caves set into the banks of the Yi River. The principal Buddha figure was fifty-five feet high. Although damaged by Western collectors a hundred years ago and further desecrated by the Red Guards in the Cultural Revolution, Longmen is still an eloquent testimony to the fervour for Buddhism which swept China from the fourth to the ninth centuries. When it finally reached its zenith under the Tang Dynasty (618–907), there were 4,500 Buddhist monasteries and a quarter of a million monks scattered throughout the Empire.

This remarkable flowering was not entirely unopposed. In both 446 and 574 there had been anti-Buddhist persecutions, often supported by the religion's Confucian and Taoist rivals. As Buddhism gained in influence and wealth it became, paradoxically, more vulnerable to attack. Why, it was asked, should a religion of ascetics, supposedly contemptuous of the world, own vast estates and control the lives of tens of thousands of Chinese peasants? Only the Chan (Zen) sect was relatively immune from criticism, hard manual labour forming an integral part of its spiritual discipline.

The 55ft high image of Vairocana, the Buddha of Ultimate Wisdom, carved at the Longmen Caves, Luoyang, China, during the Tang Dynasty.

Yungang Caves, Datong, northern China. Despite the scars left by European treasure hunters and Chinese iconoclasts most of the interior temple sculpture has remained in a good state of preservation.

Previous spread: Workers are nowadays free to worship at the Yungang Caves. Most of the caves were carved in the fifth century when Yungang became a major Buddhist centre under the Northern Wei Dynasty.

In 715, Buddhist images which contained large quantities of precious metals were confiscated, and in 729 all monks and nuns were required to register with the authorities. Resentment simmered, but not until 845 was a systematic attempt made to break the power of the Buddhist Sangha. Then the order was given to demolish all Buddhist buildings, to confiscate monastic land, to liberate the exploited peasantry and to secularise the Buddhist clergy by force.

As it turned out, Buddhism was by now far too well established to be killed off with a single blow. Its golden age was nonetheless over and the cultural pendulum swung back towards Chinese orthodoxy. For a thousand years Buddhism slowly declined. Ultimately, only two schools remained: Pure Land, with its singular emphasis on the doctrine of salvation by faith and Chan (Zen), robust, enigmatic, and by temperament indifferent to either official praise or censure.

The general estimation of Buddhism reached its nadir in the second half of the nineteenth century. The Chinese, faced with the realisation that they had been technologically superseded by the West, a state of affairs underlined by the activities of Christian missionaries, began to cast around not only for scapegoats but also for a substantial source of revenue with which to begin the task of national regeneration. In 1898, legislation was passed enabling local authorities to requisition monastery land. The law was repealed in 1906, but a precedent had been set for subsequent administrations to follow.

The first quarter of the twentieth century saw sustained attempts to generate a Buddhist revival, culminating in the foundation of the national Chinese Buddhist Association in 1929, but in 1930 only one to two percent of the population were committed lay Buddhists and the future, even without a Communist revolution, was looking decidedly bleak.

There are few places today where it is possible to imagine what Chinese society

would have been like if the Revolution had never happened. One of the few is the Wen Shu Yuan temple in the southern city of Chengdu. Due to the more liberal political climate of the past decade, Wen Shu Yuan has recently become one of the most active Buddhist centres in the whole of China. Yet the activity to be seen there is completely dissimilar to that at Fayuan Si in Beijing. Whereas Fayuan Si is a hushed, sombre place, the monks pursuing their studies isolated from the life of the city around them, Wen Shu Yuan has a fairground atmosphere and at weekends hundreds of ordinary people throng its ancient courtyards. Children play among the flowerbeds, venerable gentlemen sit reading their newspapers and a queue waits patiently for the services of an elderly fortune teller. The wooden buildings, erected in 1691, are freshly painted, their windows picked out in brilliant orange and scarlet, and in the main hall, the images are gaudy, newly gilded and wreathed by incense, coiling up in blue spirals from huge brass cauldrons. An altogether delightful place, Wen Shu Yuan provides a colourful setting for recreation as much as for ritual, the generations mingling together in tranquil conformity to immemorial patterns of social behaviour.

At the Jokhang Temple in Lhasa, overlooked by the Dalai Lama's great palace, the Potala, and by the bare, snow-streaked hills of central Tibet, the atmosphere of religious fervour is almost palpable. Road-weary pilgrims, ghostly with dust, fling themselves full-length on the ground outside the country's holiest shrine, their pious prostrations often continuing for hours. Women, faces burnt almost black by the high-altitude sunshine, weighed down by strings of rough-cut turquoise, sit impassively, steadily whirling their prayer wheels – brass cylinders invariably inscribed with the most famous of all mantras: 'Om Mani Padme Hūm – Hail to Thee, Jewel at the Heart of the Lotus'. Young Chinese soldiers in baggy green uniforms, raw recruits from the big industrial cities two thousand miles to the East, look on with incredulity and amusement. How could their reaction be otherwise?

At Yungang fifty caves have been carved out of the sandstone cliff. The largest Buddha figure is 40ft high, and over 50,000 smaller sculptures people the caves.

165

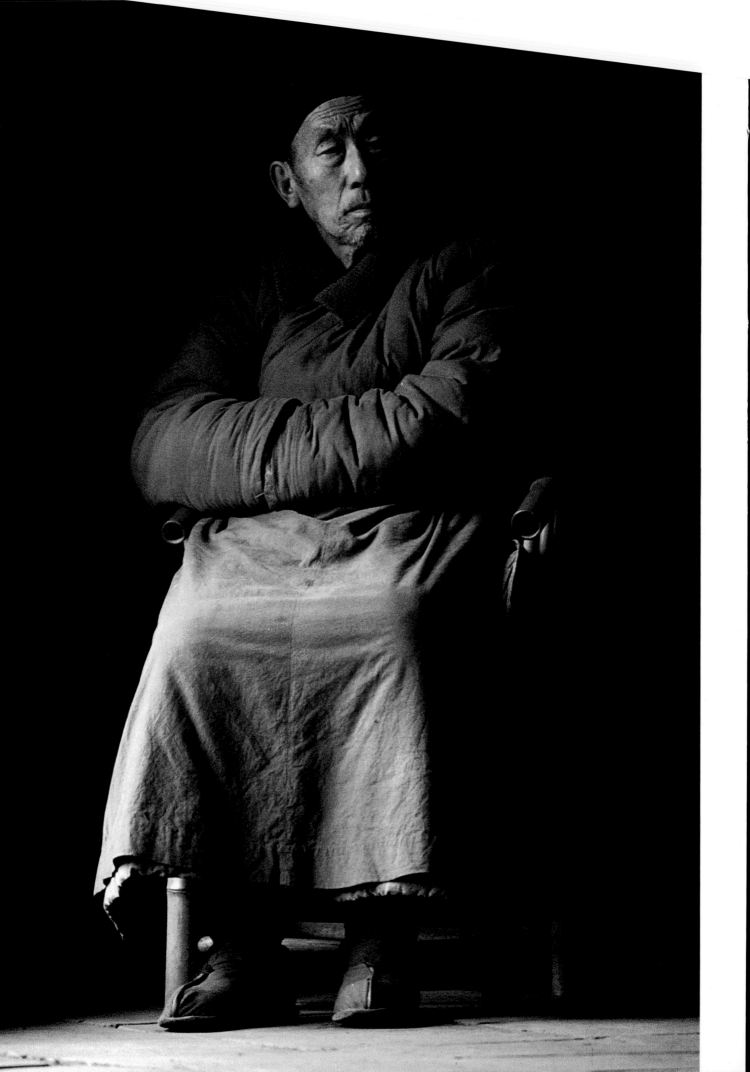

Workers attend the
evening service at Wen
Shu Yuan, Chengdu,
southern China.

Opposite: A monk keeps
himself warm and sits
guarding the entrance to
the main Dharma Hall
at Wen Shu Yuan.

Pilgrims carrying butter lamps visit a shrine within the walls of the Potala Palace, Lhasa, Tibet.

Opposite: The Potala was spared from destruction by Red Guards during the Chinese Cultural Revolution at the request of Premier Zhou Enlai.

Previous spread: The magnificent Potala Palace, Lhasa, Tibet, seen across the Kyichu River. Begun in 1645, it took forty-six years to build. It was intended as a symbol of the power of the Great Fifth Dalai Lama, the first Tibetan to combine the offices of supreme religious and political leader.

170

Left: Sitting on a crag 1000ft above the city of Lhasa the Potala Palace is silhouetted against the dawn sky.

Right: Fragments of a *khata* entangled with spring blossom at Tashilhumpo monastery in Tibet's second city of Shigatse.

Tibetan Buddhist culture is so alien to everything with which they are familiar.

Today, it is once more possible, quite openly, to buy pictures of the Dalai Lama at the stalls surrounding the Jokhang. Quite how far liberal policies will be pursued, however, it is difficult to say. The chief reason for the relaxation of restrictions may be the Chinese desire to encourage tourism by preserving Tibetan Buddhist culture as a museum piece. The Dalai Lama has already expressed his willingness to abandon claims to national sovereignty in return for the Tibetans being granted regional autonomy. Maybe such an accommodation will lead one day to negotiations undertaken in a spirit of reconciliation.

Just outside Lhasa, at Drepung, once the largest of all Tibetan monasteries with a population of around 10,000, two or three hundred monks now cling precariously to the wreckage. Many of them are young, certainly too young to remember monastic life before the invasion. For the most part, they seem ragged, demoralised and ill-educated. Obliged to make their homes in the midst of the dereliction, they often possess little more than an old mattress and two or three blankets. The walls of their

inadequate shelters are black with soot, and sacking flaps at windows shattered by explosions twenty years ago.

Five miles away at Sera, Lhasa's other great monastery, things seem a little better. At least the monks appear to be rather more adequately clothed and fed. There are also a few older lamas, men of evident stature, supervising the education of the teenage novices. Yet here too the evidence of destruction is unavoidable: tattered fragments of propaganda posters still cling to five hundred-year-old frescoes, many of which have slogans scrawled across them and the courtyard of one building is filled to a depth of six or seven feet by smashed images of the Buddha and the bodhisattvas of the Tibetan pantheon.

Opposite: A brass amulet box, worn by a pilgrim monk circumambulating the Barkhor, the sacred road which surrounds the Jokhang, Lhasa.

Following spread: Begun in 1440, the Kumbum Stupa overlooks the town of Gyantse, southern Tibet. The stupa contains some of the finest surviving examples of Tibetan religious frescos.

Hope nonetheless survives at Sera, and a modest amount of reconstruction is even taking place. On most days two or three dozen local people can be seen struggling with baskets of earth and stones, and gradually new buildings in the traditional style rise from among the ruins of the old. Certainly one could wish for no clearer demonstration of the continuing vitality of Buddhism in Tibet today. Monks and lay people are united in a common longing to see the Dalai Lama return to his ravaged country, in order that they may regain simultaneously their independence, their dignity and their freedom of religion. Whereas in China it seems unlikely that any social or political change could greatly revive the fortunes of Buddhism, Tibet remains, even in adversity, the most deeply devout of all Buddhist countries.

Prayer flags stand in the Kyichu River near Lhasa.

Opposite: A goddess makes the offering of music in a fresco on the walls of one of the temple buildings at Drepung, Lhasa.

Following spread: A Tibetan pilgrim prostrates in front of the Jokhang, Lhasa's holiest shrine. Prostrations, which may last for several hours, days or even weeks, are performed to dispel worldly pride.

177

6

*T*he Modern Movement

Buddhism comes to the West

'Preoccupation with the riddles of Zen may perhaps stiffen the spine of the faint-hearted European, or provide a pair of spectacles for his shortsightedness.'
C. G. Jung

Unlike the Western monotheistic religions, Buddhism has not been greatly discomfited by three hundred years of startling scientific discovery. There are a number of reasons for this equanimity. First, Buddhism has shown little enthusiasm for defending a cosmology which science has shown to be false. Galileo spent the last ten years of his life under house arrest for supporting Copernicus' theory that the earth revolves around the sun. The Buddha said that such subjects as the nature, or origin, of the universe were futile and the discussion of them in no way aided the release from suffering which was the purpose of his religion. Secondly, Buddhism claims to be a religion grounded in reason rather than revelation, and therefore to be compatible with the prevailing ethos of scientific rationalism. Thirdly, Buddhism has long maintained that the nature of matter and the nature of the self are completely different from the way they appear to be, attitudes which give it a vague affinity with two of the most crucial departments of twentieth-century science: relativistic physics and psycho-analysis.

Recently the extravagant claim has been made for Buddhism that it is now the fastest-growing religion in the Western world. Of course there is a good deal of difference between Buddhism's attracting the attention of a few leading Western intellectuals and its becoming a popular religion, so how much truth is there in this spectacular assertion?

The first contacts of any significance between Buddhism and the West came about as a result of European colonialism. Although the Indian Emperor Aśoka is known to have sent envoys to Greece and Alexandria in the third century BC, Buddhist ideas appear initially to have made little impression. Later, Islamic expansion throughout the Near East erected a formidable barrier between Europe and India. By the beginning of the nineteenth century, however, Eastern ideas were clearly beginning to emerge in Western thought. Schopenhauer's great work *The World as Will and Representation*, published in 1819, was influenced by both Buddhism and Hinduism, while its author is said to have kept a small gold statue of the Buddha prominently displayed in his study.

Despite his enthusiasm for Eastern religion, Schopenhauer never travelled to the Orient, so his philosophical enquiries must have been considerably hindered by the inaccurate and incomplete source material that was available at the time. It was only in the later years of his life that systematic attempts were first made to codify and to translate the huge corpus of Buddhist and Hindu scriptures. As the dominant eighteenth- and nineteenth-century colonial powers in the Far East were Britain and

Opposite: Western Theravādan monks stroll on the lawns at Chithurst Forest Monastery, Hampshire, England.

France, it is hardly surprising that scholars from these two nations should have been among the first to study the indigenous cultures in depth. In 1837 a translation of the Pāli text of the *Mahavamsa* (the *Great Chronicle of Ceylon*) was made by a British civil servant, George Turnour, and in 1844 the publication of Eugene Burnouf's *Introduction to the History of Indian Buddhism* made clear for the first time the relationship between the Pāli (Theravāda) and the Sanskrit (Mahāyāna) traditions. In 1872, another British civil servant, Robert Childers, published a *Dictionary of the Pāli Language*, and in 1881 arguably the most eminent figure in early European Buddhist studies, Professor T. W. Rhys Davies, founded the Pāli Text Society, which was responsible, over many years, for the translation of the Theravāda canon into English.

The crucial extension of Buddhist scholarship to a wider audience came in 1879 when Sir Edwin Arnold's long poem, *The Light of Asia*, an account in verse of the life and teaching of the Buddha, became a best-seller. So great was the poem's influence that another significant event can be clearly linked to its publication. In 1901 Allan Bennett, who had been introduced to Buddhism by Arnold's work, became the first Westerner to enter the Sangha. Bennett was ordained in Burma (although he had studied extensively in Sri Lanka) and took the name Ānanda Metteyya. In 1907 he returned to England, where he began the Buddhist Society of Great Britain and Ireland. This organisation survived until 1925, but by then it had already been superseded by The Buddhist Lodge (later The Buddhist Society), founded in 1924 by Christmas Humphreys.

If Buddhism's introduction to the West was initially at the instigation of Europeans, then much of the movement's subsequent impetus has come from the United States. Although some nineteenth-century American writers were influenced by Eastern ideas (most notably Henry David Thoreau who translated into English Eugene Burnouf's French edition of the Lotus Sūtra) it was not until 1893 that Buddhism first achieved widespread publicity, when a World Parliament of Religions was organised to coincide with the Chicago World Fair. The meeting was addressed by two eminent Buddhists, Anāgārika Dharmapāla from Sri Lanka, and the Japanese Rinzai Zen master, Soyen Shaku. Anāgārika Dharmapāla, famous as the founder of the Maha Bodhi Society, the organisation dedicated to the restoration of the Buddhist holy places of India, gave two speeches which stressed the many ethical similarities between Buddhism and Christianity. It was, however, Soyen Shaku who was destined to make the greater impact, albeit indirectly. At Chicago he was introduced to an American publisher in need of someone skilled at translating Japanese into English. Sōyen Shaku happened to have a young pupil, Daisetz T. Suzuki, who was suitably qualified, and arrangements were made for him to travel to America.

Suzuki's first visit lasted for eleven years. When he died in 1966 at the age of ninety-six, he had almost single-handedly made Zen Buddhism an integral part of American culture. General interest was first kindled by the publication in 1927 of his *Essays in Zen Buddhism*, but subsequently he devoted a considerable proportion of his working life to explaining Zen to Westerners in terms which he knew they would understand. Even in the 1950s, at the age of more than eighty, he was still keeping to a demanding schedule of lectures at Columbia University in New York. Suzuki's many books, including the classic *Zen and Japanese Culture*, have left an indelible impression throughout the English-speaking world, and moreover, one entirely independent of the whims of fashion.

After the Second World War, interest in the supposed connection between Oriental religious experience and the effects of psychedelic drugs such as mescalin, culminated in the phenomenon known as 'Beat Zen'. Such books as Aldous Huxley's *The Doors of*

Perception, Jack Kerouac's *The Dharma Bums* and Timothy Leary's *The Politics of Ecstasy* engendered a cultural climate where familiarity with the terms and basic concepts of Eastern religions became an indispensable prerequisite for a successful social life. Now that times have to some extent changed, it can be seen that such trivial enthusiasm probably did more good than harm: many people who today take a serious interest in Buddhism will readily admit to having been introduced to the religion during the hippy, anti-establishment era of the 1960s and early 70s.

Buddhism came to America, unlike Europe, along two completely different paths. Academic and literary interest in Britain, France and Germany was paralleled in the United States by the work of scholars and writers and by the foundation of organisations such as the First Zen Institute of America in New York in 1930. However, America faces the Pacific as well as the Atlantic and the last quarter of the nineteenth century saw large numbers of Chinese and Japanese immigrants arrive in California. Many of these people were Buddhists belonging predominantly to Pure Land sects. Despite the pressures to conform to the prevailing Christian ethos, Buddhism continues to thrive on the West Coast among the settlers' descendants. It is, however, a Buddhism which has adapted to fulfil the pastoral duties traditionally carried out by Christian denominations. Since 1944, Jōdo-shinshū (Japanese Pure Land) groups have even been organised as the 'Buddhist Church of America'.

In recent years, by far the most significant factor affecting the number of practising Buddhists in America has been the unprecedented success of the Japanese 'new religion', Sōka Gakkai. Known in America as Nichiren Shōshū, the movement is based in Santa Monica and now claims to have over half a million adherents, including one percent of the total population of greater Los Angeles. Quite why Sōka Gakkai should have become so attractive to Americans (and increasingly to Europeans) is something of a mystery. Not being a centralised, dogmatic religion has enabled Buddhism to develop many widely different traditions. Were it not for its astonishing success in making converts, Nichiren Shōshū might simply be regarded as further evidence of this fundamental tolerance of innovation. However, such an equable attitude is rather difficult to sustain when the movement's activities have been responsible for virtually all the recent publicity given to Buddhism as 'the West's fastest-growing religion'.

History has scarcely had time to form a balanced view of the cultural transformation undergone by Western societies in the 1960s and early 70s. Was it the Great Enlightenment, or the Great Aberration? All that is certain now is that things can never be quite the same again: the past can be temporarily ignored, but it cannot be entirely forgotten. The extreme liberalism of that era may have promoted self-indulgence and naivety, but it also encouraged people to look the world full in the face, without preconceptions. Thankfully that spirit of courageous re-examination has not been completely obliterated in the return to less adventurous values.

Opened in 1979, Chithurst Forest Monastery in southern England has become a notable example of something that not very long ago was regarded as an impossibility: a unit of the Buddhist Sangha functioning on European soil exactly as it would in the East. Every morning the monks go on their alms round, walking along the English country lanes with their begging bowls to houses pleased to provide them with food. There are approximately twenty-five ordained bhikkhus living in strict accordance with the Vinaya. For example they never handle money and, when they are obliged to travel, a lay Buddhist organises the purchase of tickets on their behalf. In this and all other aspects of their daily routine there is almost no difference between Chithurst and its parent monastery, Wat Nong Pah Pong, in north-eastern Thailand.

A Western monk in the apartments reserved for the use of the Dalai Lama in the new gompa at Samye Ling Tibetan Centre, Eskdalemuir, Scotland.

Previous spread: Monks practising *zazen* in the *zendō* at Throssel Hole Priory, Hexham, Northumberland, England.

The abbot of Wat Nong Pah Pong, the revered Theravāda teacher Ajahn Cha, has attracted many foreign disciples since the 1960s. To one of the most notable, an American who took the name Ajahn Sumedho, he entrusted the task of establishing an International Forest Monastery, Wat Pah Nanachat, also in north-eastern Thailand. This proved to be extremely successful. In 1977 Ajahn Sumedho accompanied Ajahn Cha on a visit to England and afterwards stayed behind to try to establish a successful Sangha. The turning point came in 1978 with the unexpected gift of 108 acres of uninhabited woodland in West Sussex – an almost perfect environment for a forest monastery on the Thai pattern. In the following year the dilapidated Chithurst House, just a few hundred yards from the entrance to the wood, was purchased and the slow process of renovation begun.

All the effort which has since been expended has unquestionably been worthwhile. Chithurst is now securely established as an international religious institution with monks from Europe and all over the English-speaking world. There is even a Laotian, seeking refuge from the bloodshed of South-east Asia. Further Theravāda Buddhist centres have sprung up elsewhere in England, including a large complex in Hertfordshire which is now Ajahn Sumedho's particular responsibility, and in 1985 two monks were sent to establish a branch monastery in New Zealand. There are apparently plans for one in Switzerland. What is impressive, however, is not so much the rapidly-increasing number of such places, but the quality of the spiritual life which is carried on there. At Chithurst, discipline is strict and conditions are spartan, yet even to the casual visitor there is an unmistakable atmosphere of harmony, one created by virtues being assiduously practised, not merely preached. Although in the past Westerners have often been accused of merely dabbling in Eastern religions, it would seem that now there are people prepared to devote their lives with the utmost seriousness to the often arduous path of Theravāda Buddhism.

Chithurst has obviously benefited from the close relationship it enjoys with a monastery in the East: it is directly in touch with an ancient tradition and is able to draw on the experience of centuries. Zen monasteries in the West have not generally been in such a fortunate position. Despite the pioneering work of people such as Dr D. T. Suzuki, it has seldom been easy for foreigners to study in Japan and to be accepted as suitable candidates for ordination. Not only are the Japanese an island people, but their country was closed to the outside world for 250 years from the seventeenth to the nineteenth centuries, a prolonged isolation which considerably exacerbated their sense of racial singularity. In view of this cultural chauvinism, and the great additional disadvantage of being a woman, the achievements of Peggy Kennett, now the Reverend Rōshi Jiyu-Kennett, are quite remarkable. Originally a student of the Theravāda Buddhism, she was ordained in the Chinese Rinzai Zen tradition at Malacca in Malaysia in 1962. Subsequently she became the first woman for centuries, of any nationality, to be admitted to Sōjiji, one of the two principal Sōtō Zen training monasteries in Japan (the other being Eiheiji). In 1969, having been given permission to teach, she founded Shasta Abbey, a Sōtō monastery in northern California, and became its first Abbess. The fierce determination and courage which must have been required to go against the grain of both Western and Japanese society can only invite admiration.

Shasta Abbey is today only one of numerous Zen institutions on the west coast of America, perhaps the best known being the San Francisco Zen Center, which opened in 1961 under the direction of the Sōtō Zen master, Shūnryu Suzuki, author of the minor classic *Zen Mind, Beginner's Mind*. Within three years of its foundation, however, Shasta Abbey had become sufficiently well established to open a branch monastery in England: Throssel Hole Priory, near Hexham in Northumberland. While both Shasta Abbey and Throssel Hole are extremely similar to a Japanese Sōtō Zen monastery, there are differences. Chief among these is the completely equal status accorded to women. In Japan, Sōtō Zen monasteries are male preserves and, once they are qualified to teach, Japanese Sōtō Zen priests are allowed to marry. At Shasta Abbey and Throssel Hole, monks and nuns live side by side, sharing the same *zendō*, where they eat, sleep and meditate. Strict celibacy is required of both men and women. Other differences are of form rather than content: the Japanese scriptures have for example, been translated into English and are chanted in a style adapted from Gregorian plainsong. Although such concessions to the Western cultural background have not always met with unanimous approval, fundamentally the Zen practice at these monasteries is as demanding as it is in Japan and great commitment and self-discipline are required from those who choose to adopt it as a way of life.

As a loose generalisation it would perhaps be true to say that the history of Buddhism in Europe has been dominated by the Theravāda tradition, whereas in America Zen has been the major influence. Theravāda travelled in the baggage of European colonial administrators, while Zen hopped across the Pacific via Hawaii. Nowadays, however, such distinctions are almost meaningless, as all the major traditions have become established throughout the West. Nothing illustrates the international character of Western Buddhism more clearly than the Tibetan diaspora which followed the escape of the Dalai Lama into exile in 1959.

The very first Tibetan centre in either Europe or America was Samyé Ling, founded in 1967 at Eskdalemuir, a tiny village in an isolated part of south-western Scotland. Two Tibetan lamas of the Kargyu School, Trungpa Rinpoche and Akong Rinpoche, had originally come to Britain in 1963 to study in Oxford at St Antony's College and the Radcliffe Infirmary respectively. Four years after their arrival, circumstances conspired to present them with a large, rambling farmhouse in the misty, green, countryside of the Scottish Borders. Rising to the challenge, they set to work. Progress initially was slow and in 1970 Trungpa Rinpoche left for America. Fortunately, Akong Rinpoche's perseverance was gradually rewarded and in 1978 Samyé Ling was sufficiently established for work to begin on a large *gompa* (temple), intended to become the focal point of a Tibetan cultural complex housing a library, lecture rooms, video and tape archives, workshops and extensive accommodation. With a working capital of just £4,000 such plans were decidedly optimistic but, a decade later, the gompa is finished. This remarkable achievement has been made possible partly by donations, but chiefly by fees from the six hundred or so people who now come to stay at Samyé Ling each year.

Although there are monks and nuns in residence, Samyé Ling is not so much a monastery as a Tibetan cultural centre; visitors can, for example, learn about traditional Tibetan painting and its associated iconography, as well as pursuing more conventional religious studies. There does, however, appear to be growing interest in the more demanding side of Tibetan Buddhist practice. In the grounds of Samyé Ling is a separate retreat centre and those who wish to commit themselves to the full rigour of religious training may embark on a nine-year course of instruction, including four years in complete isolation under the supervision of a retreat master. Such courses, apparently, are fully subscribed. Akong Rinpoche's stated aim is to make Samyé Ling the largest Tibetan centre in Europe. Given what has already been achieved, this would seem to be an entirely feasible ambition, though certainly there are a number of contenders for pre-eminence.

In England, the Manjushri Institute in Cumbria opened in 1976 under the supervision of Gelug-pa lamas, becoming the first centre in Europe to offer training up to the standard of *geshe*, or Doctor of Divinity. There are also numerous well-established Tibetan centres in a number of other European countries, particularly in France and Switzerland. Interest in Tibetan Buddhism would seem to be everywhere on the increase. This is doubtless partly due to the fact that, until the flight of the Dalai Lama and other senior Tibetan religious figures to India, little was really known about this remarkable tradition. Although some Westerners may well be attracted to Tibetan Buddhism simply because they find it exotic and mysterious, an increasing number are fascinated by its analysis of human consciousness and the sophistication of the techniques it has developed to lead the practitioner to spiritual fulfilment.

What is true of Europe is equally so of the United States. Recently there has been speculation that over the next two or three decades Tibetan Buddhism could have an impact on American culture similar to that made by Zen during the past forty or fifty years. In 1970, leaving Samyé Ling in the capable hands of Akong Rinpoche, Trungpa Rinpoche left Britain to found Tibetan centres in Nova Scotia, Vermont, and Colorado. Other Tibetan lamas have taken up residence in the United States, often in association with the major universities. The degree of the interest that they have aroused may be judged by the fact that in 1981 the Dalai Lama performed the Tantric Kālachakra Initiation ceremony to a congregation of some twelve thousand people.

'The new electronic interdependence recreates the world in the image of the global village.' It is now more than twenty years since Marshall McLuhan's epoch-making assertion. In those twenty years Buddhism has certainly consolidated its position in the West and continued to win new converts. But how significant have its advances really been? How far has Buddhism progressed towards becoming a world religion, or more specifically towards becoming the religion of the 'global village' of the future?

As well as being compatible with the scientific spirit of the twentieth century, Buddhism stresses peaceful coexistence in an age threatened by nuclear Armageddon, and proclaims the interconnectedness of all forms of life to a world increasingly dismayed by the deterioration of the environment. In many respects it seems to offer a creed uniquely suitable for our times. It speaks eloquently to those who are convinced that the future of Man will not be determined by his ability to construct ever more brilliant pieces of machinery, as it does to those who despair that we have devoted our ingenuity to the subjugation of nature, while making little effort to investigate systematically the workings of our own minds, to understanding the true reality of our existence rather than blithely accepting the convenient fiction.

Yet despite the fact that the world is perceived to be out of joint – that the intuitive and the rational, the spiritual and the material, are as far removed as ever from the desired consummation – it is highly unlikely that Buddhism, in the immediate future at least, will meet with much more widespread acceptance in the West. Indeed the interest in Buddhism shown by Western intellectuals may have a greater effect on orientals than occidentals, by fuelling the reassessment of traditional culture currently taking place in Thailand and Japan. Buddhism is a demanding religion. Belief is insufficient. Action is required. It is not enough merely to subscribe to the values which Buddhism promotes; the individual must give up time, that most valuable of resources in the modern world, so that he may spiritually progress. While many people have found that brief but regular periods of meditation can be helpful in the context of an ordinary working life, real spiritual attainment needs dedication, not dilettantism. To a far greater degree than, say, Christianity, Buddhism is in essence a monastic religion. It requires that we reassess our priorities and, to an inconvenient extent, insists that we turn our backs to the world.

Nonetheless, as the religion of a growing minority, Buddhism will continue to flourish. The Dharma has come to the West and it seems certain that it will not be extinguished. Some Europeans and Americans clearly do have the faith and the strength of will to enter the Sangha and to make a conspicuous success of their chosen life. Moreover, in societies where any kinds of consensus concerning ultimate aims and values seems unattainable, the message of Buddhism, founded in self-reliance, will remain a perennially attractive one. For the individual determined to come to terms with his own destiny, the Buddha's last words to his disciples will continue to provide an inexhaustible source of inspiration:

'O monks, I take my leave of you. All the constituents of being are transitory. Work out your own salvation with diligence.'

Following page: A Western bhikkhu meditates outside his hut at Chithurst Forest Monastery, England.

Buddhist Asia

MONGOLIA
□ ULAN BATOR

U.S.S.R.

JAPAN
□ TOKYO
KOREA   Eiheiji △ △ Kamakura
KYOTO □ Nara
Sŏkkuram
□ BEIJING   Hae' In-Sa △
△ Datong   Hwaŏm-Sa

TURKESTAN
Dunhuang △
CHINA
△ Luoyang
XI'AN □   Nanking ○
△ Jiuhua Shan

AFGHANISTAN   LADAKH
GANDHARA   ○ Leh
Dharamsala   TIBET
CHENGDU □

PAKISTAN   NEPAL   □ LHASA
DELHI □ KATHMANDU ○ Shigatse
Lumbinī △ □ △ Gyantse
Kusinārā △ ○ Darjeeling
Varanasi ○ △ Sārnāth
△ Nālandā
Bodh Gayā △

Sāñcī △
△ Ajanṭā   ○ Mandalay
△ Ellora   △ Pagan
BOMBAY □   Chiangmai
INDIA   BURMA   △ Ban Chiang
△ Si Satchanalai
RANGOON □ △ Sukhothai
THAILAND
BANGKOK □ △ Angkor

Mysore ○

△ Suan Mokh

△ Anurādhapura
△ Polonnaruwa
COLOMBO □ ○ Kandy
SRI LANKA

INDONESIA

JAVA △ Borobudur

When Buddha died in about BC 463 his religion had strictly local influence. Its development into a major cultural force throughout the East took place haphazardly over many centuries. The most crucial factor was the patronage of the Indian Emperor Aśoka in the third century BC during whose reign Buddhism spread throughout India and the sub-continent and became established in Sri Lanka. By the twelfth century, it had virtually disappeared from India. However, in Japan it was at its apogee, while in Tibet its golden age was yet to come.

As Buddhism has no centralised authority, there has been little effort to convert the adherents of other religions: nor has there been a planned programme of expansion. When it was at its height in India (c. third century), scholars travelled from all over Asia to the monastic universities which flourished there.

Mahāyāna Buddhism is often referred to as the 'Northern School' and Theravāda as the 'Southern School', although these terms can be misleading. Today Theravāda thrives in Sri Lanka and South-east Asia, while the Buddhism found north of the Himalayas is chiefly of the Mahāyāna type. However, for centuries Hinayāna (Theravāda) and Mahāyāna Schools existed side by side.

KEY TO MAP
□ CITIES
○ TOWNS
△ BUDDHIST SITES

193

Glossary

A note on language

Buddhist scriptures have been recorded in, or translated into, many languages, most notably Pāli (P), Sanskrit (S), Chinese (C), Japanese (J), and Tibetan (T). The fundamental terminology of the religion is common to both the ancient Indian languages of Pāli and Sanskrit, sometimes with minor variations in spelling: for example Dhamma (P), Dharma (S); Kamma (P), Karma (S). In this book the spelling has been chosen which is most appropriate in the specific context. Pāli is the language of Theravāda Buddhism; Sanskrit that of Indian Mahāyāna.

Abhidhamma (P) The third collection of the Theravāda Canon, the Tipitaka (q.v.), containing doctrinal and philosophical systemisation of Buddhist doctrines and practices.

Amida (J) See *Amitābha*.

Amitābha (S) 'The Buddha of Boundless Light', worshipped in devotional Chinese and Japanese schools. Sincere faith in him is said to ensure rebirth in the Pure Land, or paradise of Sukhāvatī (q.v.).

Anattā (P) One of the 'Three Signs of Being' and a cornerstone of Buddhism, being the doctrine that as nothing in man is immune to the universal law of impermanence he consequently has no soul.

Anicca (P) One of the 'Three Signs of Being'; the universal law of mutability or impermanence.

Arahat (P) See *Arhat*.

Arhat (S) The spiritual ideal of early Buddhism; a perfected man who attains Enlightenment and escapes from the cycle of rebirth.

Avalokiteshvara (S) The Bodhisattva of Infinite Compassion; the embodiment of one of the two great concepts of Mahāyāna Buddhism (q.v.): Karunā (q.v.) and Prajñā (q.v.).

Bhikkhu (P) A Buddhist monk whose life is governed by the discipline of the Vinaya (q.v.).

Bodhi (S) Enlightenment.

Bodhisattva (S) The spiritual ideal of Mahāyāna Buddhism (q.v.). A person who, having attained Enlightenment, is motivated by compassion to remain within the cycle of rebirth and thereby to further the liberation of all living beings.

Buddha (S/P) A Fully Enlightened Being; one who has awakened to a Supreme Understanding of spiritual deliverance.

Buddhi (S) The faculty which enables man to achieve Supreme Understanding.

Chan (C) The Chinese word for 'meditation'. It became the name of a Buddhist school which concentrated on methods by which 'the Buddha-mind of Enlightenment' might be generated. Known in Japan as Zen (q.v.).

Chenrezi (T) The Tibetan name for the Bodhisattva Avalokiteshvara (q.v.); the Dalai Lama is regarded as one of his manifestations.

Dhamma (P) See *Dharma*.

Dharma (S) A word of immense significance and considerable complexity, having a variety of meanings, the most important and frequently encountered being 'the Teaching of the Buddha'.

Dukkha (P) One of the 'Three Signs of Being' and the first of the 'Four Noble Truths'. Given that man has no immortal essence and that he is inescapably subject to the law of impermanence, he experiences the unsatisfactory nature of life as dukkha, which may be loosely, and somewhat inadequately, translated as 'suffering'. The remedy for this condition is the Buddha's Dharma (q.v.).

Gautama (S) Buddha's clan name.

Gelug-pa (T) One of the four principal schools of Tibetan Buddhism, founded at the beginning of the fifteenth century by the reformer Tsong-kha-pa. The Dalai Lama is a Gelug-pa, but nowadays he is regarded as the spiritual leader of *all* Tibetans. The head of the School is the Abbot of Ganden monastery near Lhasa.

Geshe (T) The title given to a Tibetan Buddhist monk who is successful in examinations at the conclusion of many years of study. Approximately equivalent to the degree of Doctor of Divinity.

Gompa (T) A Tibetan Buddhist monastery.

Gotama (P) See *Gautama*.

Hīnayāna (S) The so-called 'Lesser Vehicle of Salvation', a pejorative title bestowed on the early Buddhist schools by the later Mahāyāna (q.v.). The only surviving Hīnayāna school is the Theravāda (q.v.).

Jiriki (J) Salvation by personal effort, as opposed to Tariki (q.v.). These terms provide a useful means of categorising the many Japanese Buddhist schools.

Jōdo (J) The Japanese name for the Chinese Ching-t'u or 'Pure Land' school of Buddhism, brought to Japan in the twelfth century by Hōnen. The school believes that good works, devotional practices, and devout faith in Amida Buddha (q.v.) are sufficient to secure salvation.

Jōdo-shinshū (J) See *Shin*.

Kamma (P) See *Karma*.

Kanjur (T) The first collection of the Tibetan Buddhist Canon, comprising the scriptures attributed to the Buddha himself. Conventionally it consists of 108 volumes containing Vinaya (q.v.), some early Sūtras (q.v.), Mahāyāna scriptures, and Tantras (q.v.). These texts are translations from Indian languages, mostly Sanskrit.

Kargyu-pa (T) One of the four principal schools of Tibetan Buddhism, founded in the eleventh century by the teacher, Marpa and which places great emphasis on meditation. Marpa's most famous pupil was the yogic poet Milarepa.

Karma (S) The ancient Indian law of cause and effect, common to both Hinduism and Buddhism. At root the word means simply 'action', but in Buddhism it generally indicates action of a moral or immoral character. In this way Karma becomes the moral law of the universe by which men reap good for good, or evil for evil. The idea is linked with that of rebirth – effects thereby being indissolubly related to causes across the apparent divide of death.

Karunā (S) Compassion. One of the two great concepts of Mahāyāna Buddhism (q.v.), the other being Prajñā, (q.v.).

Kegon (J) The Japanese name for the Chinese Hua-yen School of Buddhism. Its teaching centres around the Avatamsaka, or 'Flower Garland' Sutra, described as the culmination of Mahāyāna Buddhist thought. Although a relatively small Japanese Buddhist school, its influence has been completely disproportionate to its size.

Kōan (J) In Rinzai Zen Buddhism (q.v.), a word or phrase not easily analysed, set as a subject for meditation with the intention of thereby freeing the mind from the limitations of the intellect. The religious awareness which thus becomes possible is first experienced as a sudden illumination known as satori (q.v.).

Lama (T) A senior member of a Tibetan Buddhist order. Some particularly important lamas, such as the Dalai Lama, are regarded as reincarnations of their predecessors in an identifiable spiritual lineage.

Mādhyamika (S) The 'Middle Doctrine' school of Indian philosophy, crucial to Mahāyāna Buddhism (q.v.), and which was founded by Nāgārjuna in the second century AD. Its central concept is that the true nature of all things is shūnyata (q.v.), or 'emptiness'.

Mahāyāna (S) The self-proclaimed 'Great Vehicle of Salvation', also known as the Northern School. Mahāyāna first came into being in India as a gradual development from the earlier Hīnayāna schools (q.v.). It is highly speculative and mystical and may most crucially be distinguished from the Hīnayāna by its view of the Buddha as the embodiment of a Transcendental Reality, rather than as a unique historical personage. Mahāyāna stresses the importance of compassion in addition to wisdom, and consequently has for its ideal the bodhisattva (q.v.), as opposed to the arhat (q.v.).

Maitreya (S) The Buddha of the Future. Both Theravāda (q.v.) and Mahāyāna (q.v.) Buddhism predict the appearance of another Supremely Enlightened Being.

Mandala (S) A sacred diagram with a highly complex esoteric meaning, used as a map of spiritual reality to be followed by the mind in meditation.

Mantra (S) An invocation, the repetition of which is held to have magic powers or to be conducive to religious awareness.

Mudrā (S) Ritual gestures of the hands endowed with symbolic meaning.

Nembutsu (J) Mantras used by Pure Land and Nichiren schools of Japanese Buddhism. The constant repetition of these is said to ensure rebirth in the paradise of Amida Buddha (q.v.). The concentration generated by repetition induces a state of heightened consciousness.

Nichiren (J) Japanese Buddhist School founded by the controversial thirteenth-century reformer, Nichiren. There are today various Nichiren sects, most notably Nichiren Shōshū, the name given in the West to the Soka Gakkai movement. Central to all Nichiren groups is a belief that the name of the Lotus Sūtra has immense mantric power and that the constant repetition of it is capable of generating the highest Enlightenment.

Nirvāna (S) Final liberation from the bonds of existence. An unconditioned state outside the cycle of rebirth. Nirvāna is ineffable, therefore to consider it as a form of extinction is a misconception. Theravāda Buddhism (q.v.) tends to regard Nirvāna as an escaspe from suffering, whereas in Mahāyāna (q.v.) it is viewed more positively as the final realisation of the Buddha-nature potential in all of us.

Nyingma-pa (T) One of the four principal schools of Tibetan Buddhism, said to have been initiated by Padmasambhava in the eighth century AD.

Prajñā (S) The highest state of transcendental wisdom. One of the two great concepts of Mahāyāna Buddhism (q.v.), the other being Karunā (q.v.).

Rinzai (J) One of the two principal schools of Zen Buddhism, also known as the 'Sudden School' due to its emphasis on the use of kōan (q.v.) and the experience of satori (q.v.).

Sākyamuni (S) Sage of the Sākyas. A title given to the Buddha, his father being ruler of the 'Sākya' people.

Sākya-pa (T) One of the four principal schools of Tibetan Buddhism, based on the teachings of the mystic Drogmi and named, in the eleventh century, after the great monastery of Sākya. Unlike the other schools, the office of leader of the Sākya-pa is hereditary.

Samathā (S/P) A type of meditation designed to develop concentration or one-pointedness of mind.

Samsāra (S) The interminable cycle of rebirth, the Wheel of Life, from which the Buddha's Dharma (q.v.) provides a means of escape.

Sangha (S/P) The monastic community founded by the Buddha, the members of which are bound by the rules of the Vinaya (q.v.).

Satori (J) In Rinzai Zen (q.v.) a flash of illumination, a sudden access to Truth, which may vary in duration. This state of religious awareness is by no means the end of the spiritual quest. The practitioner must learn to sustain the revelation; to live within the Reality which he has so dramatically perceived.

Shin (J) Abbreviation of the Jōdo-shinshū, the 'True Sect of the Pure Land', founded early in the thirteenth century by Shinran as a modification of the Jōdo School (q.v.) of his teacher Hōnen. Shin is a devotional school of Buddhism relying exclusively on the invocation of the name of Amida Buddha (q.v.). It is today the largest Buddhist school in Japan.

Shingon (J) The Japanese esoteric 'School of the True Word', founded by Kukai at the beginning of the ninth century. It is greatly influenced by Tantric (q.v.) beliefs and practices.

Shūnyatā (S) Emptiness. The most fundamental idea in Mahāyāna Buddhist philosophy, particularly systematised and interpreted in the Mādhyamika School (q.v.) of Nāgārjuna. It is the dominant theme of the vast Prajñā-pāramitā (Perfection of Wisdom) literature. 'Emptiness' is the closest approximation that language can provide to the ineffable Ultimate Reality.

Skandha (S) The five components – body, feelings, perceptions, volitions and consciousness – which, in the Buddhist analysis, go to make up a living being. Being casually conditioned they do not individually or collectively constitute a separate self or ego.

Sōtō (J) The larger of the two main Japanese Zen (q.v.) schools, brought from China by Dōgen in the twelfth century. Unlike those of the Rinzai Zen school (q.v.), Sōtō practitioners do not employ kōan (q.v.).

Stūpa (S) Originally a large mound, built over cremated remains of the Buddha, but later one containing relics of revered Buddhist teachers or sacred books.

Sukhāvati (S) The paradise, or 'Pure Land', of Japanese Jōdo (q.v.) and Shin (q.v.) schools of Buddhism, in which the devotees of Amida Buddha (q.v.) hope to be reborn. As well as being interpreted literally, Sukhāvati may be thought of as a beatific state of consciousness.

Sūtra (S) Discourses of the Buddha. The second section of the Canon of the Theravāda School (q.v.), the Sutta Pitaka, may well contain the Buddha's own words. The Mahāyāna (q.v.) Sūtras, although attributed to the Buddha, are believed by scholars to be the work of later writers.

Sutta (P) See *Sūtra*.

Tan (J) The raised platform, covered in tatami matting, round the walls of a zendō (q.v.) on which Zen monks sleep, eat, and meditate.

Tanhā (P) Desire, the will to live; a crucial link in the chain of Dependent Origination binding man to the cycle of rebirth.

Tanjur (T) The 'Translation of the Treatises', the second part of Tibetan Canon, containing 225 volumes of commentaries on both Sūtras (q.v.) and Tantras (q.v.).

Tantra (S) A category of scriptures which advocates a form of highly complex, esoteric religious practice. Tantras are found in both Buddhism and Hinduism. The dates and authorship of the various texts are disputed. Tantra is today chiefly encountered in Tibetan Buddhism, where meditation and ritual are combined to provide a 'short path' to salvation. One of the most important and controversial aspects of Tantra is its transformation of the power of sexual desire in order to eliminate obstacles to the Mind of Enlightenment.

Tantrayana (S) 'Tantric Buddhism'. A form of Buddhism which developed on the basis of the Tantras and which considers itself to be much more effective than its predecessors, the Hīnayāna and the Mahāyāna.

Tariki (J) Salvation brought about by the intervention of an outside power, usually Amida Buddha (q.v.), as opposed to that gained by Jiriki (q.v.).

Tendai (J) Extremely important Japanese school of Buddhism, founded by Saicho in the early ninth century on Mount Hiei near Kyoto. It derives much of its inspiration from the Lotus Sūtra and emphasises the importance of meditation.

Theravāda (P) The Doctrine of the Elders and the only surviving early Buddhist school. Preserved in Sri Lanka, it eventually spread to the whole of South-East Asia and is consequently known as the Southern School. It is based on the Pāli Canon, or Tipitaka (q.v.).

Tipitaka (P) The 'Three Baskets' of the Pāli Canon, the scriptures preserved by the Theravāda tradition (q.v.). These are the Vinaya Pitaka (q.v.), the Sutta Pitaka (q.v.) and the Abhidhamma Pitaka (q.v.).

Tum-mo (T) A form of meditation in Tibetan yogic practices which enables the practitioner to generate 'vital heat'. On a religious level, this heat is used to 'melt' the obstacles to Enlightenment. It can, however, also be employed in a thoroughly practical manner, enabling hermits to survive the Himalayan winter in the most spartan of conditions.

Vinaya (S/P) The first of the three divisions of the Tipitaka (q.v.) concerning the rules of discipline for the Sangha (q.v.).

Vipassanā (P) 'Insight Meditation'. Unlike samatha (q.v.), it is said to be a type of meditation discovered by the Buddha, a discovery which enabled him to come to his realisation of the Ultimate Truth, or Enlightenment.

Yogācāra (S) An important school of Indian Mahāyāna philosophy, founded in the fourth century by the brothers Asanga and Vasubandhu. It is also known as the Mind-Only school because of its central assertion that the phenomenal world does not, in absolute terms, really exist, being only a manifestation of mind or consciousness. The truth of this point of view, the school maintains, can be experienced through meditation.

Zazen (J) Zen meditation.

Zen (J) A form of Japanese Buddhism concerned with the achievement of the Buddha-mind of Enlightenment, principally through meditation. The word 'Zen' means meditation. It is derived from the Chinese Chan School, which was itself said to have been brought from India in the sixth century by Bodhidharma. There are two principal Zen sects in Japan today: Sōtō (q.v.) and Rinzai (q.v.).

Zendō (J) Large hall in a Zen monastery where the monks eat, sleep and meditate. It is consequently the centre of their lives.

Bibliography

1 The Noble Path

Bechert, H., and Gombrich, R., **The World of Buddhism**, London, 1984.

Conze, E., **Buddhist Scriptures**, London, 1959.

Conze, E., **A Short History of Buddhism**, London, 1982.

Dumoulin, H., and Maraldo, J. C., **Buddhism in the Modern World**, New York, 1976.

Humphreys, C., **A Popular Dictionary of Buddhism**, London, 1976.

Murti, T. R. V., **The Central Philosophy of Buddhism**, London, 1955.

Snellgrove, D. L., **Indo-Tibetan Buddhism**, Boston and London, 1987.

Stryk, L., **World of the Buddha**, New York, 1968.

2 First Principles

Bunnag, J., **Buddhist Monk, Buddhist Layman**, Cambridge, 1973.

Mascaro, J., **The Dhammapada**, London, 1973.

Rahula, W., **The Heritage of the Bhikkhu**, New York, 1974.

Rahula, W., **What the Buddha Taught**, London, 1978.

Smith, D. E., **Religion and Politics in Burma**, Princeton, 1968.

3 The Buddha-Mind

Byron Earhart, H., **The Religions of Japan**, San Francisco, 1984.

Herrigel, E., **Zen in the Art of Archery**, London, 1985.

Leggett, T., **A First Zen Reader**, Tokyo, 1960.

Sansom, G. B., **Japan: a Short Cultural History**, Tokyo, 1973.

Suzuki, D. T., **An Introduction to Zen Buddhism**, London, 1983.

Suzuki, D. T., **Zen and Japanese Culture**, New York, 1959.

Wilson Ross, N., **The World of Zen**, New York, 1960.

Wood, E., **Zen Dictionary**, London, 1977.

4 An Open Secret

Chang, G. C. C., **Songs of Milarepa**, Boulder and London, 1977.

Govinda, Lama Anagarika, **Foundations of Tibetan Mysticism**, London, 1969.

Harvey, A., **A Journey in Ladakh**, London, 1983.

Hopkins, J., and Lati Rinbochay, **Death, Intermediate State and Rebirth**, London, 1979.

Hopkins, J., **The Tantric Distinction**, London, 1984.

Snellgrove, D. L., and Richardson, H., **A Cultural History of Tibet**, Boston and London, 1986.

Snellgrove, D.L., **Buddhist Himalaya**, Oxford, 1957.

Tucci, G., **Theory and Practice of the Mandala**, London, 1969.

Tucci, G., **The Religions of Tibet**, London, 1970.

5 Decline and Destruction

Avedon, J. F., **In Exile from the Land of Snows**, New York, 1984.

Blofeld, J., **The Wheel of Life**, London, 1959.

Fitzgerald, C. P., **China: a Short Cultural History**, London, 1986.

Harrer, H., **Seven Years in Tibet**, London, 1955.

H. H. the Dalai Lama, **My Land and My People**, New York, 1962.
Richardson, H., **Tibet and its History**, Boston and London, 1984.
Van Walt van Praag, M. C., **The Status of Tibet**, London, 1987.
Wright, A. F., **Buddhism in Chinese History**, Stanford, 1965.

6   *The Modern Movement*

Fields, R., **How the Swans Came to the Lake**, Boston, 1986.
Humphreys, C., **Both Sides of the Circle**, London, 1978.
Oliver, I. P., **Buddhism in Britain**, London, 1979
Snelling, J., **The Buddhist Handbook**, London, 1987.
Watts, A., **In My Own Way**, New York, 1973.

Acknowledgements

We have been helped by many people in England, and throughout the Far East, since our work on this book began in 1984. In particular, we wish to extend our grateful thanks to the following for their help and advice:

England
Celia Clear, Suzannah Gough, Rachel Rogers and Julie Young, British Museum Publications; Susan Mann, the book's designer; Ajahn Munindo and the Ven. Vagiro, Chithurst Forest Monastery, Petersfield, Hampshire; Ken Holmes, Kargyu Samye Ling, Eskdalemuir, Dumfriesshire; and the Rev. Roshi Daishin Morgan, Throssel Hole Monastery, Hexham, Northumberland. In addition we would like to thank Martin Sillwood of Japan Airlines; Claudia Rosencrantz; Audrey Harrison; Ben Williams; Mike Gilmore; and Linda Rose.

Burma
Ashin Thriya, Thiri Mingala Monastery, Botataung, Rangoon.

The People's Republic of China
Madam Sun Geng Xin and Mr Wong, Ministry of Culture, Beijing; Shi Leng Xing, Fayuan Si, Beijing; and Martin Davidson, British Council, Beijing.

India
Mrs Sushma Bahl, British Council, New Delhi; Mr Foy Nissen, British Council, Bombay; Mr P. A. Nazareth, First Secretary, Indian Council for Cultural Relations, New Delhi; Dr M. S. Nagaraja Rao, Dir. General and Mr M. D. Khare, Dir. (Monuments) Archaeological Survey of India, New Delhi; and Dr A. P. Jamkhedkar, Dir. Archaeology and Museums, Bombay.

Tenzin Geshe Tethong, Private Secretary to His Holiness the Dalai Lama; Kalon Tashi Wangdi, Representative of His Holiness the Dalai Lama in New Delhi; Denma Locho Rinpoche, Abbot, Ven. Kelsang Damdo and Yogi Pembo, Namgyal Monastery, Dharamsala.

Japan
Mrs Toshiko Nishida MBE, British Council, Tokyo; Mr Naohachi Usami, Kyoto; Mr Takashi Hamada, Dir. General, Mr Shinya Inagaki, Curator in Chief, and Mr Fujita, Nara National Museum, Nara. Kanehara Toei, Ichi Ryu Hattori, Kobayashi Shugaku, Kuniyasu Daichi, and Brant Reiter, Eiheiji.

Korea
Mr Han Churl Mo, National Museum, and Mr Jim Hoare, British Embassy, Seoul.

Nepal
Lisa Choegyal, Tiger Mountain Travel, Kathmandu; Mr Alec Patterson, British Council, Kathmandu; Mrs Diki Dolkar, Office of the Dalai Lama, Kathmandu; and Mr H. R. Auerbach, Pan Am.

Sri Lanka
Mr Ladauhetty, Permanent Secretary, and Dr Roland Silver, Dir. General, Central Cultural Fund, Ministry of Cultural Affairs, Colombo; Mr Marcus Gilbert, Assist. Rep. and Dr Rajiva Wijesina, PR, British Council, Colombo; Ven Kondanna, Ven. Piyaratana and Bhikku Maha Thera, Island Hermitage, Dondanduwa.

203

Thailand
Ven. Buddhadasa Bhikku, Suan Mokh, Chaiya; Ven. Phramaha Bang Khemananda, Wat Parelai, Ban Chiang; Ven. Pharmaha Somsak Sambimb, Wat Pra Chetubon, Bangkok; Chatsumarn Kabilsingh Ph.D., Associate Professor, Faculty of Liberal Arts, Thammasat University, Bangkok; Mr Somkind, Fine Arts Dept., Bangkok; Khun Euayporn Kerdchouay, Siam Society, Bangkok; Miss Maneerhat, Deputy Director, Sukhothai Historical Park, Sukhothai; and Valerie Teague, British Council, Bankok.

Photographic Information

All the photographs in *Living Buddhism* were taken by Graham Harrison on two Nikon FM2 cameras using the following Nikkor lenses: 15mm f5.6, 18mm f3.5, 24mm f2, 35mm f2, 55mm f2.8 Macro, 105mm f2.5, 80-200 f4 Zoom, and 300mm f4.5.

The film stock used was Kodak Ektachrome 64 Professional, Kodak Ektachrome Tungsten 50 Professional, and Kodachrome 64 Professional. E6 processing was done by East West Colour Laboratories, Tokyo, Japan; E6 Company Ltd., Bangkok, Thailand; Far East Laboratories, Tokyo, Japan; Kodak (Far East) Ltd., Hong Kong; and Lancaster Laboratories, London, England.

All photographs in the book are the copyright of Graham Harrison, except those of Korea, on pages 90–95, which are reproduced by kind permission of the Telegraph Sunday Magazine.

Abhidhamma 28, 29, 137
Ajahn Chah 75, 186
Ajahn Sumedho 186
Akong Rinpoche 187–8
alms 29, 66, 72
Ambedkar, Dr B.R. 10
Amida Buddha 34, 100, 102, 103
Amitābha 34
Anagārika Dharmapāla 13, 182
Ānanda 19–20, 29, 73
Ānanda Metteyya 182
Anathapindika 18
anattā 23
Anawratha 53
animal life 24, 45
arhat 28, 34
Asanga 35
Aśoka 20, 42, 45, 180
Aung San, General 56
Avalokiteshvara 110

Bandaranaike, S.W.R.D. 47
Bangkok 62, 72
Beat Zen 182–3
Bennett, Allan 182
Bhikkhu Buddhadasa 75
bhikkhu *see* monks
Bodh Gayā 14, 18
Bodhidharma 88, 89
bodhisattva 34, 100
Brahmins 13
Buddha
    death 19–20
    Enlightenment 14, 23, 32
    life 13–14, 18–20
    teaching 18–19, 23–5, 28, 85, 100
Buddha Gautama *see* Buddha
Buddhism (see also) Chan; Mahāyāna;
        Theravāda; Tibetan Buddhism;
        Zen
    contemporary 10, 12, 39
    decline 12–13, 38
    expansion in Asia 20, 23, 98
    fundamentals 10, 14, 18, 23–5, 28,
        189
    and the laity 38–9
    and politics 10, 12, 45, 47, 56, 59,
        104
    revival 13, 164
    western view of 10, 12–13, 182
    and women 73

as a world religion 188–9
Buddhist Councils 28, 56
Buddhist Society 182
Burma 53, 56, 59, 62

Chan 88, 89, 161, 164
Chih-i 99
Childers, Robert 182
China
    Buddhism in 13, 88, 146, 147, 154,
        164–5, 172
    coming of Buddhism 154–5, 160–1
    suppression of Sangha 144, 161–4
    and Tibet 146–7, 165, 172
Chithurst Forest Monastery 183, 186–7
community development projects 72–3
Confucianism 155, 160
Cultural Revolution 110, 144, 147

Dalai Lama
    ceremonial duties 113, 128, 133, 188
    and monastic life 136, 141
    optimism for the future 110, 112,
        120
    relations with China 146–7, 172
    relations with the laity 112–13
    as religious and national leader 110,
        113, 117
death 23, 120
Deity Yoga 25, 124
desire 23
Devadetta 19
Dhamma *see* Dharma
Dhammapada 46
Dharamsala 110, 112, 113, 141
Dharma 18, 23, 28, 100, 189
Diamond Sutra 35
discipline, monastic 29, 72, 82
Doctrine of the Elders 28
Dogen 82, 84, 102
Drepung 133, 136, 172
dukkha 23

education
    of the laity 52, 72, 136
    of monks 66, 133, 136–7
Eiheiji 78, 81–2, 84, 107
Eisai 99, 102
Elders, the 28, 29
Emptiness 35, 89, 161

Enlightenment
   of the Buddha 14, 32, 85
     pursuit of 81, 88, 89, 100, 102, 103
Eskdalemuir 187
Essays in Zen Buddhism 182

Fayuan Si 144, 146, 165
forest dwellers 47, 52, 75
Four Noble Truths 18, 23–4, 28

Ganden 133, 136, 147
gardens, Zen 91, 96
Gelug-pa 116–17, 136
geshe 137, 188
gods
   and Buddhism 38, 52, 120, 123–4,
     128
   Shinto 98, 100
gompa 188
Great Britain 180, 182, 183, 186–8

Heart Sūtra 35, 81
Higher Dharma 28
Hīnayāna 28, 32, 35, 124, 125
Hinduism 34, 38, 52
Honen 100, 102
Hui-kuo 100
Humphreys, Christmas 182
Hyakujyo Nehan 81

India 12, 13, 32, 38
initiation ceremonies 128, 133, 188
Insight meditation 25
*Introduction to the History of Indian
   Buddhism* 182
invocation 102
Islam 12, 23, 38, 180
Itivuttaka 46

Japan
   growth of Buddhism 89, 91, 98, 99
   monasteries in 78, 81, 82, 84, 187
   Zen gardens 91, 96
Japanese Buddhism (see also) Jodo;
   Nichiren; Zen
   82, 84, 98, 99, 100, 105, 107
Jetāvana Grove 18–19
jiriki 102
Jōdo 100, 102, 103
Jōdo-shinshū 102, 183
Jokhang Temple 165

Jōsei Toda 107

Kālachakra 128, 188
Kamakura 91
kami 98, 100
Kanishka 20
Kanjur 124
Kargyu-pa 116
karma 23
karunā 34
Kassapa 29
Kathmandu Valley 38
Kennett, Peggy 187
kōan 91, 96
Kondañña 18
Kūkai 100
Kumarājīva 161
Kusinara 20
Kyoto 91, 99

laity
   in monasteries 66
   relations with Sangha 38–9, 66, 72
land tenure, monastic 42, 47
Lao Tsu 155
Light of Asia, The 182
Lin-Chi 89
Longmen 161
Lotus Sūtra 35, 99–100, 103–4, 107,
   161
Lumbinī 13

Mādhyamika 34–5, 89, 123, 137, 161
magical beliefs 100, 123
Maha Bodhi Society 182
Mahākāshyapa 85, 88
Mahānikāya 63
mahāvairocana 100
Mahāvihāra 45
Mahāyāna
   canonical literature 124
   growth of 28, 32, 38, 52–3, 125
   principles 32, 34–5
Mahinda 45
mandalas 25, 107
Manjushri Institute 188
mappō 100, 103
material prosperity 98, 112, 147
meditation
   by laity 62
   purpose 28, 81, 120, 123

techniques 25, 78, 96, 128
merit 59
Middle Doctrine 34
middle way 14, 35
Milarepa 141
Mind 35, 123
Mindon, King of Burma 56
monarchy and the Sangha 45, 56, 59,
   63, 66
monasteries
   Tibetan 133, 137, 141, 172
   Western 183, 186, 187, 188
   Zen 78, 81, 82, 84, 91, 187
Monastery of the White Horse 154
Mongkut, King of Thailand 63, 66
monks
   discipline 29, 72, 82
   as educators 52, 72, 136
   novices 81–2, 136–7
   occupations 52, 72–3, 133
   political activity 56, 59
   routine 78, 81–2, 84, 133, 136, 183
Mount Hiei 99, 100
Mount Kōya 100
Muslims *see* Islam
Myōshin-ji 91

Nāgārjuna 34–5
Nālandā 12
nats 59
Ne Win, General 59
nembutsu 102
Nichiren 103–4, 107
Nichiren Shōshū 104, 105, 107, 183
Nikkō 104
Nirvāna 28, 66, 125
no-self, doctrine of 23
Noble Eightfold Path 24–5, 28
nuns 187
Nyingma-pa 116

oral tradition 29

Padmasambhava 116, 123
Pagan 53, 56
Pāli Text Society 182
Pancha Sila 24
Perahera Festival 52
Perfection of Wisdom 35, 137
Phenpo Drupthop 141
physical work 81

pilgrims 82, 165
politics and Buddhism 10, 12, 45, 56,
   59, 104
Potala Palace 110, 117
prajna 34, 137
Pure Land 34, 100, 103, 104, 164

Reality 18, 32, 85, 89, 102, 123
rebirth 23, 120, 123
recluses 141
reincarnation *see* rebirth
religious persecution 10, 12, 38, 144,
   147, 161, 164
Rikon 128
Rinzai 89, 91, 96, 102
Rōshi Jiyu-Kennett, Reverend 187
Ryōanji 96, 98
Ryōbu Shintō 100

Saichō 99
Sakya-pa 116, 117
samatha 25
Sammā Samādhi 28
samsara 23
Samyé Ling 187, 188
San Francisco Zen Center 187
Sangha
   in China 144, 146
   features 19, 29–32, 39, 160
   and the monarchy 45, 56, 59, 63, 66
   origins 18, 19
   and politics 45, 56, 59
   in society 66, 72–3
Sārnāth 18
satori 85
Schopenhauer, Artur 180
science and Buddhism 110, 180
Self, the 19
Sera 133, 136, 172
sexual behaviour 24
shakubuku 107
Shākyamuni 13, 39, 84–5
Shasta Abbey 187
Shin 102, 103
Shingon 100
Shinran 100, 102
Shintō 98, 100, 105
Shūnryu Suzuki 187
Shūnyatā 35
Shwedagon 42
Siddhārtha 13–14, 18 (see also) Buddha

socialism and Buddhism 56, 59
Sōka Gakkai 105, 107, 183
Sōtō Zen 78, 81, 82, 89, 91, 102, 187
Soyen Shaku 182
spirit world 123
Sri Lanka 13, 45, 46–7, 52, 63
Suan Mokh 75
subconscious, the 25
suffering 23
sūtras 35
Sutta Nipāta 20
Suttas 29, 46
Suzuki, Dr Daisetz T. 91, 182, 187

Taizōin 91
Tamils 45
tanhā 23
Tanjur 124
Tantra 38, 99, 125, 128, 133
Tantrāyana 25, 35, 125, 128
Tantric Buddhism see Tantrāyana
Taoism 155
tariki 102
Tendai 99, 100, 103
Thailand 10, 62–3, 66, 72–3, 75
Theravāda
    in Burma 53, 56, 59, 62
    canonical literature 29, 45–6
    monks 29, 52, 66, 72–3
    origins and purposes 29, 52–3
    in Sri Lanka 45–7, 52
    in Thailand 62–3, 66, 72–3, 75
    and the West 32, 187
Three Baskets 46
Three Jewels 18
Throssel Hole Priory 187
Tibetan Buddhism, and the West 120,
    188
Tibet
    adoption of Buddhism 23, 123
    and China 146–7, 165, 172
    magical beliefs 123
    Mongol influence 117
    and the West 120, 188
Tibetan Book of the Dead 120
Tibetan Buddhism
    canonical literature 124–5, 128
    and the laity 10, 154
    monastic culture 133, 136–7, 141,
        172
    origins 116

principles 38, 120, 123
    and the West 120, 188
Tibetan Tantric Buddhism 25, 35, 125,
    128
Tipitaka 45, 46, 59, 75
tranquillity 25
True Pure Land 102
True Word 99
Trungpa Rinpoche 187–8
Truth 96, 100, 103
Tsao-tung 89
Tsong-kha-pa 116, 117, 147
tum-mo 123

U Nu 56, 59
U Ottama 56
U Wizaya 56
Ultimate Reality see Reality
Ultimate Truth 100, 103
United States 182, 183, 187, 188
Universal Absolute 34
Upali 29

Varanasi 18
Vasubandhu 35
Vinaya 29, 75, 137
vipassanā 25
Virtuous Ones 117
visualisation 123

Wat Nong Pah Pong 183, 186
Wat Pah Nanachat 186
Wen Shu Yuan 164–5
Western world
    growth of Buddhism 183, 186–9
    view of Buddhism 10, 12–13, 120
    writings on Buddhism 180, 182–3
wisdom 24, 34, 85
With Mystics and Magicians in Tibet 123
women, Buddhism and 73, 187

Yogācāra 35, 123

Zen (see also) Chan; Rinzai; Sōtō Zen
    growth in West 107, 182, 187
    and Japanese culture 98
    monasteries 78
    origins 35, 88, 89, 91, 164
    principles 85, 88, 89
Zen and Japanese Culture 182